Virgin VEGAN

THE MEATLESS GUIDE ♥ to PLEASING your palate

LINDA LONG

GIBBS SMITH
TO ENRICH AND INSPIRE HUMANKIND

To the elegant and endearing and forever friend, Walter Feldesman. What an overwhelming honor to be called his friend.

And,

To the people who started my journey when I was a virgin vegan . . .

The brave civil rights activist Dick Gregory and his personal intent that I should see the value of the vegan way and change my life's direction.

Dr. Michael Klaper, a one of a kind doctor and friend. His star shines so brightly to so many, yet so many have yet to know his open heart and teachings.

Sun and Light and Sky of Gentle World who gently influenced me in ways they never knew and which resonates still.

First Edition
16 15 14 13 12   5 4 3 2 1
Text © 2012 Linda Long
Illustrations © 2012 as noted throughout
Photographs © 2012 Linda Long
Photographs © 2012 Anita Lombri 108, 124, and 157

The publisher nor the author claim to be a nutritionist, a scientist, or a medical doctor. The author's authority on the subject is based solely on personal experience and research. Note that nutritional data changes with new research.

Published by
Gibbs Smith
P.O. Box 667
Layton, Utah 84041

1.800.835.4993 orders
www.gibbs-smith.com
Designed by AJB Design
Printed and bound in China
Gibbs Smith books are printed on either recycled, 100% post-consumer waste, FSC-certified papers or on paper produced from sustainable PEFC-certified forest/controlled wood source. Learn more at www.pefc.org.

Library of Congress Cataloging-in-Publication Data

Long, Linda, Date–
   Virgin vegan : the meatless guide to pleasing your palate / Linda Long. — 1st ed.
      p. cm.
   Includes index.
   ISBN 978-1-4236-2516-2
1. Vegan cooking. I. Title.
   TX837.L627 2012
   641.5'636—dc23
                        2012015350

Contents

THANK YOU!

Virgin Vegan: The Meatless Guide to Pleasing Your Palate started when I picked up the phone one day and on the other end was Gibbs Smith, Christopher Robbins, and Jennifer Adams with an idea for this book. After *Great Chefs Cook Vegan* required photographing 25 chefs in 13 cities, I was over the adventure of book making for a while. But, their idea was a book for beginners, filled with just the information needed for a fast start. I would be able to take photos, my greatest fun, and even give brand names of ingredients, just like I do when having conversations around New York City with someone who asks what to do. This was very exciting!

I made a brief outline based on our four-person phone call, and we were set. My mind immediately thought of everyone who guided me when I was uncertain about what to do for meals and shopping, and how to live in a world with little agreement about what I wanted to eat, or rather, not eat.

Mid-stream, my kind editor, Michelle Branson, jumped in to head the project. I thank her so much, and appreciate her trust in my vision for the book, even when it was not originally hers. It soon became ours. She surprised me with the title!

Linda Lombri is a longtime friend, and writer of her own book. I felt so much support from her at every turn. I call her my pre-editor! She might call herself my therapist.

Food photography has its own special requirements beyond point and shoot. I was so lucky to have Catherine Molitor to style many of the shots in this book. She always came with a good spirit and tons of creativity. With some shots I had the help of Claire Wiegand, who even carried five heavy squash on the subway. Thanks to Anita Lombri for styling several dishes along with her fine food photography, the only other "shooter" in this book.

Being video interviews are an extension of this book, I had to learn to shoot and edit video. See **www.virginvegan.com.** My learning curve was made shorter by Molly Higgins, who seems born to edit, and knows how to teach—a real talent. Although I am so grateful to Mellissa Mallow, who first patiently taught me how to retouch photos over the phone, Molly sat with me and gently gave the gift of confidence in my photo retouching skills as well. Big thanks to both young women!

A recipe book requires testers. No matter how great a cook, when it comes to publishing a recipe book, testers are a must. Thanks especially to home economists Jane Belt and Rhonda Martinez who did many recipes with little notice. Huge thanks to Sarah Ott, Tommy Oaks, Dotti Kauffman, Bobbi Boock, Tom Boock, Alice Sprout, Lazarus Lynch, Roger Tappen, and Dilip Barman for being willing to test no matter what the recipe.

I wanted the book to reflect not only my cooking style but also the dishes of others I admire. As you go through the book, you will find wonderful recipes from many people who love to cook and also do great things in the world. Their names are with their recipes. Grandiose thanks to all!

To be sure of the medical or nutritional information, I consulted the highest experts. You will see them listed on many pages. More information about them, their books, and their work can be found on **www.virginvegan. com.** Dr. Michael Klaper was especially generous and helpful with his vast wisdom. And, thanks to Dr. T. Colin Campbell for a few fast answers.

Some friends are simply great supporters. Writing a book can bring out the whiney side and I need to thank those who remain friends in spite of me . . . Linda Lombri, Inger Lonmo, Fran Costigan, Sharon Van Vechten, Josephine Hall, my sister Aileen Sharar, Sarah Lewis, Victoria Moran, Robin Asbell, Joanne Black, Zuelia Ann Hurt, Alice Frazier, Dotti Kauffman, Sandee Garihan, Caryn Hartglass, Paula Al-Sabah, Dusty Stamper, Debra Wasserman, Freya Dinshah, and especially, Walter Feldesman.

The staff at Trump Place listened to my daily laments and showed interest in this book for over a year of days, even checking on me when not seen for a long time. Warm thanks to all the staff, but especially Gaby Szathmary, Rick Martinez, Carlos Medrano, Gretchen Martinez, and doorman Steve Rush.

I know the staff at Gibbs Smith is seldom seen, but their fine work is! I wish to thank Brad Farmer for his vision of using video interviews as an extension of this book; Dan Moench for making the video website possible; Suzanne Taylor for her vision of great books; Jill Schaugaard for her enthusiastic public relation efforts, Andrew Brozyna for his creative design; and, of course, Gibbs Smith whose willingness to trust his authors makes it worth working with him.

INTRODUCTION

MY PERSONAL JOURNEY TO BEING VEGAN

"Okay, but I will only eat liver or ham because I cannot see any blood or fat!" said a determined nine-year-old girl—a compromise to her mother in hopes of never again hearing the statement, "Young lady, you sit there until every bit of that meat is off your plate!"

I was that girl. I am way older now and have not eaten animal products for decades. But, as a teen and growing up in a truck stop near Chambersburg, PA, I served and ate burgers, halibut, and hot roast beef sandwiches.

My journey with food expanded when I went on to study Home Economics at Mansfield University and Penn State where I learned how to prepare food properly and to teach it. As a student teacher, I taught my first lesson on how to make a white sauce. In those days, I could not imagine a grocery list without milk, butter, eggs, and white bread, and I gave that guideline to my students.

In my first year of teaching in Lancaster County—Pennsylvania farm country—I began to question the source of the nutritional information I taught. I noticed that most of my resources came from the Meat and Dairy Council or the USDA, both of which had a keen interest in meat and dairy production, thus a slanted point of view.

By my mid-twenties, I shifted to the fashion industry and was working in New York City. I continued to eat an animal-based diet. Among my peers, to have a steak was "the thing," a symbol that we had made it to the big time. I forgot about my food thoughts back in Lancaster County.

A decade later, I met someone who inspired me to change my diet. I was married and living at The Concord Hotel in the New York Catskills. The great Dick Gregory—comedian, civil rights activist, and self-taught nutrition expert—was there with Mohammad Ali who was training for a fight. Dick was juicing for Ali to keep his immune system up to peak performance. One day I asked him, "Can you really be vegetarian and healthy?"

We sat at a sunny window, with a book from the government that contained the nutritional breakdown of all our foods. At the end of that conversation, I was a vegetarian. Well, almost. I continued to eat Dover sole until I looked down at my plate and realized I had no appetite for it. I was done. Forever.

It was clear to me that I was not giving up anything. I was simply choosing other foods. My brain made the switch ahead of my habits.

It was clearly the health aspects that mattered to me initially but I was surprised when the thought of harming an animal for a meal hit me hard. The more I learned about the brutality of breeding and preparing animals for market, the more I could not be part of it. I realized the only difference between the animal on the plate and a pet was that one had not been named and petted. From the animal's point of view it is the same, pet or not.

My journey to vegan took a little longer. Dairy products still found their way to my table. A call from dear friends Sun and Light from *Gentle World* asking me to house their friend for one night while in New York City changed my opinion. That friend turned out to be the truly incomparable Dr. Michael Klaper, who ultimately became my teacher, inspiration, and dear friend.

I took advantage of his visit to ask about dairy and why it should not be ingested. From his growing up years, he knew a lot about the subject, and as he elaborated, I grasped his point that the milk of cows was not really designed for human consumption. But, this was one step I was not ready to take. He told me to know the facts and then choose.

The next morning, I looked at the milk I was about to pour into my morning coffee and thought to taste it without milk. After all, I grew up in a truck stop and served lots of strong black coffee. To my surprise, I liked it better. I had no need to buy milk at all.

I was thinking more purely now about food and what I would put into my body. It was both an intellectual and an emotional decision. I was vegan!

See **www.virginvegan.com** for more information about veganism, resources, videos, and more recipes!

GOOD THINGS TO KNOW–ABOUT BEING VEGAN

WHY?

POWER! The power of the fork. How else can one person affect one's health, attack animal abuse, and honor our responsibility for the Earth in one act? This is really something! All this while enjoying superb eating and even feel a bit giddy-good about it.

HEALTH

It usually starts with one reason. For me, it was for a healthier me. Respectable medical sources support the facts that a whole foods plant diet:

lowers cholesterol

lowers blood pressure

assists in managing or preventing many cancers

lessens or heals hypertension (heart disease)

lessens Type 2 diabetes

supports better weight balance

Plant foods offer important fiber, which is unavailable in animal products. This is often a surprise to people just starting to study nutrition. It is also difficult to get a balance of necessary nutrition when focusing mostly on animals for intake.

We know dairy is a real issue for so many and to intake a natural substance made to grow a small calf to a huge animal is too strong for our human bodies. No animal continues to need milk after the weaning period, and calcium is not synonymous to milk just as protein is not synonymous to meat. Both are more readily available in many whole plant foods without the harmful aspects.

This book is filled with health-related reasons for abiding by plants. What more do we need to know when we have a cure for heart disease and can prevent or reverse it, and the same for diabetes and obesity? This is amazingly the answer to most health care costs.

ANIMALS

The overuse of animals causes terrible cruelty to beautiful sentient beings. The demand is so great, even strangely glamorized, that the need to breed them, give them a heartlessly cruel life, then kill them, all seems to consider them no more than an inanimate object, to be selfishly treated in any way at all. People seem to mindlessly follow the practices of their family and friends and not do their own thinking. Once someone does, there seems to be an insight that creates another way of being. Mindless eating ends, for good.

Often fish is considered exempt from this thinking, but Heidi Etter, MS, Marine Biology, states that over fishing is killing off our ecosystem and contributing to an imbalance in the fish population through the overhaul in the nets. A hook in the mouth causes pain, and if the gills are damaged, fish cannot breath. Add to this horror is the disastrous bi-catch—other beings caught in the nets like turtles, sea birds, dolphins, sharks, and eels. The dolphins can drown in the nets. So do sharks after their fins are cut off for soup and they're tossed back in. And if that is not enough, some Asian countries use dynamite to retrieve tuna and salmon, killing many other species as well. Why should we support such destructive behavior?

ENVIRONMENT

Most people never think about meat as destroying the environment, yet it is one of the most significant reasons:

massive deforestation for grazing lands
mountains of fossil fuels
pollution of the waters
chemical absorption into the land
grain used up for animal feed
waste disposal capacity
energy consumption that drives global warming

Furthermore, meat production can't keep up with population growth, and it is driving health care costs way up! This is not a sustainable practice.

(See **www.worldwatch.org/node/549** or any writings by John Robbins.)

WHAT DO VEGANS EAT?

If it falls off a tree or grows up from the ground, it is a plant food. That's it!

The categories of plant foods fall into these groups:

VEGETABLES

All of them! Carrots, sweet potatoes, kale, and all greens are especially nutritious but all vegetables are filled with nutrients, including various amounts of protein, calcium, vitamins A and B and more. This fact that vegetables offer protein is a surprise to many.

FRUITS

All of them! Blueberries, apples, bananas all have super nutrients, such as vitamins A and C, potassium and more, but the selection is as vast as the markets. Treat your taste buds and try a new one each shopping trip. All fruit can be eaten raw so it's truly instant food and a travel food already in its wrapping.

GRAINS

All of them! You might think of wheat or rice first, and then oats, but among the most nutritious and versatile is quinoa (keen-wah) with all the amino acids of protein you need. Then consider spelt, barley, farro, kamut, and on and on and on. The great thing about grains is that they are mostly cooked the same way in prep for a great dish. Just add water and a dash of salt to a saucepan, followed by the grain, often in a 2:1 ratio of water to grain, but always check for each grain. Bring to a boil, cover, reduce heat, and cook until water is absorbed. Easy!

SEEDS

All of them! One might think seeds are not such an advantage. Seeds can produce oil, such as sesame oil, flaxseed oil, sunflower oil, and many more. Tahini is made from sesame seeds and is high vitamin C. Flax can be used for baking as substitute for eggs and for its oil that provides omega-3s. Then, there is the snacking factor, think sunflower seeds, pumpkin seeds, and hemp seeds or sprinkle over salads. They have lots of protein and vitamin E to go around, along with minerals and antioxidants.

NUTS

All of them! The most popular nut, peanut, is actually a bean/legume. Walnuts and almonds are considered especially nutritious and easy to find, but it seems every nut has its own gifts.[*]

LEGUMES

All of them! Often a source of protein over the centuries for many cultures, legumes (such as beans, lentils, peas, soy, peanuts, to name a few) also provide tons of fiber for good digestion. Beans and rice is a popular combination in several cuisines. Soybeans are the basis of tofu and tempeh. Lentils (red or brown, usually) are used in soups, salads, and spreads.

The vast volume of dishes that can be made from this list is infinite. Famed Chef Jean-Georges Vongerichten once told me that there are only so many ways to prepare animal products, but when considering plant foods, a chef can go wild with creativity when thinking about the vast selection.

9 PRODUCTS TO KNOW

You already know the most common plant foods as you have always eaten them. Here are 9 important products you might not know about and need to.

NUTRITIONAL YEAST

It is a yellow, flaky, powdery substance that is mostly used to create a cheesy taste in dishes and sold in a large container in health food stores. Although considered a supplement, it is used as an ingredient in recipes. It is a good source of omega-3s, protein, B vitamins, and fortified with B-12. Since it is deactivated yeast, free from any Candida Albicans yeast, it poses no problem for anyone with a yeast health issue. Use it to sprinkle over vegetables, salads, popcorn, and to make wonderful cheese-like sauces. See Spreads, Sauces, Dips, and Toppings for some recipes (pages 132–139). A popular brand is NOW Nutritional Yeast Flakes, Vegetarian, **www.nowfoods.com**. (Brewer's yeast is not a substitute for this.)

BRAGG LIQUID AMINOS

An alternative to soy sauce and tamari, it is derived from soy protein, and is

---

[*] Dr. Michael Greger shares extraordinary information delivered in a delightful tone on his site, **www.nutritionfacts.org.**

gluten-free. It has 16 amino acids, and has naturally occurring sodium (no salt added). If a less salty taste is desired, it can be diluted with water. It is sold in health food stores, better grocery stores, or at **www.bragg.com/products.**

TAMARI

It is actually soy sauce and means liquid pressed from soybeans. It is made with whole soybeans, sea salt, water, and a fermentation process that creates a soft but richer and smoother balance in taste. It is usually wheat-free, unlike regular soy sauce. See **www.edenfoods.com** for organic.

SHOYU

It is the Japanese name for soy sauce and is actually regular soy sauce made with half soybeans and half wheat, salt, and a fermentation process. It has a sharper taste than tamari. See **www.edenfoods.com.**

NAMA SHOYU

It is raw or unpasteurized soy sauce that allows living enzymes to remain. It is rich and full-bodied, but yet delicate in smell. Do not keep in a hot place as it continues to ferment and can expand, as it is a living food.

TEMPEH

It is a fermented soybean product that can be flavored to the dish's theme and used in any way meat is used, whole or crumbled. Keeping the whole soybean intact, it is less processed than tofu so it retains more protein, vitamins, and fiber. Some have grains or vegetables added. Look for shrink-wrapped packages of the firm, flat cake measuring about 7 x 2½ x ¾ inches. Lightlife is a popular brand, **www.lightlife.com.** See The Other Proteins (page 105).

TOFU

It is the process of coagulating soy milk and pressing into soft blocks. There are two types; silken (softer Japanese style), **www.morinu.com,** and regular (firmer Chinese style), **www.nasoya.com.** Having little flavor, it is porous enough to take on any flavoring. Used to make sauces that reflect oils or dairy, and for meatier-textured items as a meat replacement. See The Other Proteins (page 105).

SEITAN

It is wheat gluten that has the texture of meat or chicken made by over-working wheat dough. High in protein, it can be flavored to suit any dish, but can be bought already flavored in shrink-wrapped packages in boxes. Westsoy is a popular brand, **www.westsoytofu.com**. See The Other Proteins (page 106).

ENER-G EGG REPLACER

It is a white powdery potato starch mixture that acts like eggs in baking recipes when mixed with a small amount of water, **www.ener-g.com.**

AGAR (SOMETIMES LISTED TWICE, AS AGAR AGAR)

It is a tasteless jelling agent extracted from algae and used to substitute for gelatin (which is always animal-derived) in recipes. It comes in powder, flakes, or a bar. If using powder, it is an equal exchange for gelatin. Otherwise, consider that 1 tablespoon of flakes equals 1 teaspoon of powder. To set about 2 cups of liquid, use 2 teaspoons powder, or 2 tablespoons flakes, or 1 bar (7 grams), more, if liquid is high acidity, **www.edenfoods.com.**

ORDERING FROM A MENU IN A MAINSTREAM RESTAURANT

Many restaurant chains now have vegan options. If not, ask your waiter questions in the most pleasant way as they are not responsible for the menu but can help you. Remember, everyone is just where they are at the moment. At one point, we were not vegan.

APPROACH 1

"Are the vegetarian items also free of dairy and meat broth?" Often, non-vegan waiters and chefs do not consider dairy or hidden meat or chicken broth an issue. Sometimes, restaurants use the term vegetarian when they also mean vegan as well.

"Are there any vegan items on the menu?" Sometimes, it is easier to ask since more restaurants need to serve vegans, and they are becoming accustomed to answering the question.

If nothing is on the menu, *"Does the chef have a dish for vegans that might not be on the menu?"* *"Would you mind asking him?"* This is especially important as more and more restaurants have dishes for vegans that are not on the menu . . . yet . . . but chefs are ready nonetheless.

If still no acceptable response from that particular waiter (who might not know for a variety of reasons), politely ask. *"Would it be possible to speak to the chef?"*

Results can be better if you say what you want instead of what you do not want. A statement like, "I do not eat any animal products" immediately creates a question about what you do eat. It is helpful to say, "I am a vegan and do not eat animal products. Is it possible to get a meal of vegetables, beans, rice (grains can be vague), or fresh greens and such?" This starts a helpful conversation.

APPROACH 2

Approach a menu as if it were your home pantry.

Look at the sides first.

Consider the ones that might be vegan and ask about them. The concern is the use of butter instead of oil, or cheese that can be eliminated. Sometimes bacon is added to some vegetable sides, or something is sautéed or soaked in meat or chicken broth.

Look at all the items that are being served with animal entrées, perhaps rice, pasta, beans, other grains, or other vegetables.

Once these are considered and some items chosen, ask if you can be served the rice with the beans, or the pasta with a few sides, and so on. Create a meal from the menu; one that only you can see is there.

Suggestion: If there is confusion from a waiter, and it is a busy Saturday night kitchen, simply ask for the items you want, served separately, and ask for an empty dinner plate, assembling at the table. Being helpful gets faster service.

THE BEST KIND OF MAINSTREAM
RESTAURANTS FOR THE WIDEST VARIETY

Asian : Thai, Chinese, Vietnamese—ask about fish sauce then use
   soy sauce

Middle Eastern : hummus, baba ghanouj, tabouli, and more

Indian : ask for the non-butter and non-cheese items

Greek : great large beans in tomato sauce, ask about butter or broth

Italian : pasta primavera or puttanesca sans anchovies, sautéed spinach

Mexican : tostadas, checking that refried beans are animal free

AT A HIGH-END RESTAURANT

To get the best meal, be sure to tell the reservationist, "There is a vegan on the reservation, and if you could be kind enough, please let the chef know a day or so before as I have learned they like to know for the advanced shopping." Sometimes, even the reservationist is not aware of this. Then, after the meal, write a little note back to the chef in thanks before you leave.

TRAVELING? NOT A PROBLEM!

Inger Lonmo, a world traveler as a cruise ship director, has faced all possible scenarios when communicating with waiters and chefs in another language.

Consider your food needs as much as your clothing needs.

WHAT TO SAY TO A WAITER OR CHEF

The chart Inger created for these experiences helped solve the problem for her. Not only does it bring a smile, but it clears any confusion since all the animals and fish (and even the milk and eggs) are crossed off with a red X. Since some think calamari is alright, she added the squid as well. See page 16 and copy and laminate it, or print it from **www.virginvegan.com,** for your travels.

Even in foreign countries most front-desk clerks speak some English. Ask them to write in the local language, *"Kindly know that I do not eat any animals, juice of animals, fish, eggs, cheese, butter, or milk. Is it possible to have a meal with some of these ingredients; vegetables, fruits, grains, beans, soy products or nuts? I am grateful."*

It is important to mention animal juices as many do not consider chicken or beef broth to be an issue. And, many countries only know this as juice, not broth.

WHAT TO CARRY THROUGH SECURITY IF FLYING, DURING THE TRIP, AND UNTIL YOUR FIRST MEAL

Travel Kit with snack baggies each filled with:

Raw vegetables : freshly cut celery, carrots, jicama, apple slices, etc.

Dried fruit : raisins, dates, goji, berries, etc.

Grains : quinoa, rice, etc. mixed with nuts and diced vegetables, dressing

Beans, lentils : edamame, lentil salad, or hummus in a spice jar-size container as it is considered a solid

Nuts : any kind, 3-ounce containers of nut butters, best not to take peanut butter on public transport because of the allergy factor

Seeds : pumpkin, sunflower, etc.

Cereals : granola, favorite dried cereals

Crackers : whole grain filled with herbs or flaxseeds, etc.

Sandwiches : See Sandwiches-On-the-Go (pages 122–126) for ideas, pack lettuce-type items in separate place and add when eating; pack in hard container to preserve shape and reuse for return

Burgers : pack a frozen veggie or bean burger in a bun with lettuce, tomato, mustard, relish, as it will be thawed when needed. No need to heat, really.

Milk : soy, rice, almond in individual containers; 3-ounce soy yogurts. Individual containers of milk and juice are usually about 8 ounces, over the limit if flying. Take in checked luggage in a ziplock bag.

Sweets : dairy-free 70% cocoa bar and energy bars, as travel selection is limited

Fluids : carry in lightweight containers or buy after security

Take-out on the way : Peacefood Café's Eric Yu says that customers order their travel needs frequently.

More . . . consider this list and have it inspire your own list!

It is a warm thought to know that your carry-along is the best place to eat. For cruises, Inger suggests:

Speak to the chef in the morning to see the menus for the day and choose the vegetables from each dish. Ask them to hold the butter even if the food is cooked in water or oil as often they add butter at the end for flavor and not consider that to be a problem. Be nice when asking and not sharp or demanding.

When approaching someone for a special favor, it is effective to start the sentence by saying, "Is it possible?" Immediately that reference hits their thinking as something they are to actually consider and take an extra second to ponder. When abruptly asking, "I want . . ." or "Can I have . . . ?" it is easier to respond negatively as a knee-jerk reaction. I have observed this many, many times. It is a slight difference that has more than slight results.

Call ahead to be sure the ship or hotel will have soy milk available. It is amazing how easy it is to ask for the chef's desk at a hotel and leave a message with the request and arrival date.

If going to a conference, request vegan meals when registering. When you get to your table at the conference, get the attention of your waiter and mention that you are the vegan at the table so they know who you are ahead of time. If no arrangements were made, get to your table early and talk with your waiter, perhaps off to the side. It is awkward to try to explain with many dinner mates listening and it is too lengthy a time to wait until the kitchen can catch up to a special meal when serving so many diners. You might get your food when everyone else is done. Also, if handled in advance, the meal is better than what could be unseasoned and over-cooked vegetables or a fruit plate.

At your destination, ask the front desk for the local fresh market or health-food store and stock up for your needs during the trip and for the return. I love visiting local supermarkets in other areas as they reveal so much about the people. Many hotels have little refrigerators for a modest fee. I always carry my granola (see recipe on page 41) and individual soy milks for breakfast and buy bananas locally to have on hand in order to have breakfast in my room. Most granolas in hotels have refined sugar and there is usually no soy milk.

MEAL PLAN TEMPLATE

Since I never used any meal plan I was ever offered, I figured you might not as well. Perhaps a template will provide better guidance. See my ideas and create your meals based on your likes, time, and kitchen talent.

BREAKFAST

See Breakfast Power (pages 40–45) and Drinks For All Reasons (pages 46–52) for some recipe suggestions.

> *Main* : *Dry cereal*—Cheerios, Grape-Nuts, and health-food store brands with least sugar and no honey, like Uncle Sam, soaked oats; *Cooked cereal*—oatmeal, 1-minute or steel cut, or quinoa or other grains, with a pinch of salt; *Smoothie*—Imagine any mix of fruit (banana, blueberries), greens (spinach, kale) and add a liquid (dairy-free milk, juice, or water) and seeds (ground flax or hemp); *Waffles or Pancakes*—quick recipe versions, pure maple syrup (grade B), "butter" (Earth Balance), added berries, crispy

vegan bacon; *Tofu Scramble*—crumbled tofu with onions and side of potatoes, meat substitutes (tempeh bacon, sausage).

Fruit : *Dried*—add to cold cereals or to cooking water (prunes, cranberries, raisins); *Fresh*—add any to smoothies (banana), on-the-run (apple), sliced (orange) with any breakfast.

Bread : *Whole grain toast or bagel*—sprouted grain is best (Ezekiel 4 :9 found in freezer), top with nut butters (almond, cashew, peanut), "butter" (Earth Balance), or jam.

Add-ons : *Nuts*—chopped nuts (walnuts, almonds) added to cereal, pancakes, or with a smoothie.

Drinks : *Teas*—green, fruit, or spicy*; Dairy-free milks*—soy, almond, rice, hemp, oat; hot chocolate, hot milk with blackstrap molasses; *Juices*—freshly squeezed (orange), any kind purchased with added water to thin.

LUNCHES

Soups : *Vegetable* with added proteins (beans, lentil, barley).

Grains : *Whole grains*—bread, crackers or tortillas; quinoa, rice, or other grains added to most dishes.

Sandwiches or wraps : *Choices*—vegetables, tofu or tempeh, meat substitutes, hummus, avocado, mayo, mustard; *Burgers*—bean, veggie, "chicken," barbecue style.

Pizza : *Frozen*—(Amy's or Tofurky) with added toppings (spinach, onions, peppers, mushrooms, olives, vegan pepperoni).

Salads : *Basic*—greens (arugula, kale), vegetables (peppers, tomatoes), nuts.

Dressings : *Creamy or vinaigrette*—see basics in The Creative World of Dressings (pages 54–55); squeeze of lemon, lime, or orange; sprinkle of nutritional yeast or Parm Sprinkle (page 136).

Drinks : Seltzer water with lemon; green smoothie; vegetable juices.

Desserts : Soy, coconut, or cashew-based ice cream; purchased or homemade pudding; mixed fruit salad or berries.

DINNERS

Meat Alternatives : Gardein and other brands of chicken- and beef-style items; tempeh, tofu, or seitan dishes; grilled portabella

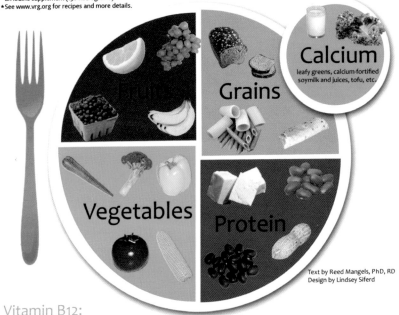

Nutrition Tips:
*Choose mostly whole grains.
*Eat a variety of foods from each of the food groups.
*Adults age 70 and younger need 600 IU of vitamin D daily.
  Sources include fortified foods (such as some soymilks) or a vitamin D supplement.
*Sources of iodine include iodized salt (3/8 teaspoon daily) or
  an iodine supplement (150 micrograms).
*See www.vrg.org for recipes and more details.

Vegan
MY ^PLATE

Calcium
leafy greens, calcium-fortified
soymilk and juices, tofu, etc.

Grains

Vegetables

Protein

Text by Reed Mangels, PhD, RD
Design by Lindsey Siferd

Vitamin B12:
Vegans need a reliable source of vitamin B12. Eat daily a couple of servings of fortified foods
such as B12-fortified soymilk, breakfast cereal, meat analog, or Vegetarian Support Formula nutritional yeast.
Check the label for fortification. If fortified foods are not eaten daily,
you should take a vitamin B12 supplement (25 micrograms daily).

Note:
Like any food plan, this should only serve as a general guide for adults.
The plan can be modified according to your own personal needs. This is not personal
medical advice. Individuals with special health needs should consult a registered
dietitian or a medical doctor knowledgeable about vegan nutrition.

VRg The Vegetarian
Resource Group P.O. Box 1463 Baltimore, MD 21203 www.vrg.org (410) 366-8343

mushrooms; nut roasts; "meat" loaf; burger patties with gravy.

Sides : Alexia frozen potato options (sweet potato fries, mashed,
etc.); Fresh greens; frozen or fresh vegetables of any kind,
lightly sautéed, steamed, or roasted; grains (brown rice,
quinoa).

Salads : Any greens or mix, dressing of choice, added beans, lentils,
add-ons like nuts, onions, peppers, cucumbers, etc.

Drinks : Water with lemon or lime, coffee, tea, vegan-friendly beer
or wine.

Desserts : Cookies, pie, cake, pudding, soy yogurt with fresh fruit, chocolate truffles, ice cream sundae.

SNACKS

Fruit : apple or other fresh fruit; dried fruit
Nuts : any kind, raw or very lightly toasted (page 140)
Herb tea : intense and refreshing (spicy, green)
Crackers : whole grain
Chips : baked tortilla or veggie chips
Salsa : purchased or homemade
Energy bars : like Clif Bars, or Addictive Energy Bars (page 157)
Popcorn : my favorite—with nutritional yeast (page 140)
Hummus, with crackers (page 142)
Soy yogurt
Carrot slices, celery sticks
Kale chips (page 144)
Guacamole
Frozen grapes (page 144)
Edamame (page 143)
70% dark chocolate : (free of any milk solids or whey)
There's no end to the choices!

BASIC PREP FOR YOUR VEGETABLES, GREENS, GRAINS, NUTS, AND BEANS

VEGETABLES

Steaming

Equipment: saucepan or skillet, lid, stainless steel collapsible steaming basket to put into a saucepan, tongs or cooking spoon

Insert a collapsible steaming basket into a saucepan large enough to allow a lid to fit tightly.

Fill bottom with water to just below the basket. (If no basket, add about ¼ inch of water and pinch of salt to the pan.)

Add vegetables, cover, bring to a boil and steam for about 3–5 minutes.

Remove the lid aimed away from you to avoid steam.

Remove vegetables immediately. (Otherwise, the steam will continue to cook even with the heat turned off.)

Sautéing

Equipment: skillet, tongs or cooking spoon

Add ¼ inch of water or stock to a skillet; or lightly coat with oil.

Set temperature to medium heat.

Add vegetables; if using larger pieces, cover initially just to heat through (sweat) and slightly soften, about 2 minutes, then remove lid to finish cooking. For medium-to-finely chopped pieces, add according to needed cooking times, such as carrots, potatoes, onions first then items like broccoli and peppers, and lastly tomatoes and mushrooms. Leafy greens need the least time.

Do not over stir or over cook as the heat within the vegetables will continue to cook a bit once heat is off.

Roasting

Equipment: baking sheet, silicon mat or parchment paper, tongs or turner

Preheat oven (or toaster oven) to 425 degrees.

Cut vegetables into the best sizes for the recipe.

On a baking sheet, place a silicon mat or parchment paper; or coat with oil.

For mixed vegetables, add the sturdiest vegetables to get a head start. Add additional vegetables after about 10 minutes. Test with fork.

Blanching

Boiling very briefly, perhaps 30 seconds, brings out the brightest colors; serve nearly raw at room temperature. Use with sturdy vegetables, like carrots, green beans, and asparagus.

GREENS

Equipment: See Vegetables above

Steaming

Same as Vegetables above.

Note that greens wilt quickly and reduce in size. Use large amounts and cook a very short time, preserving the vivid green color.

5 to 6 cups of raw leafy greens can reduce to about 1 cup of cooked greens.

Greens are filled with super nutrients and need to be cooked correctly to preserve them. They have more vitamin A than carrots, more C than oranges, more E than whole wheat, and they contain quality protein, not to forget calcium and magnesium, which is better than in fruit, seeds, and nuts.

Sautéing

Same as Vegetables above

Raw (preparing for salads)

Fill a bowl with water or partially fill a sink.

Gently stir greens to allow any grit to fall to the bottom.

Skim greens from the surface and spread onto a towel and tenderly blot or gently roll in the towel or put into a salad spinner to dry.

Store in refrigerator at least 15 minutes or more to crisp before serving. Or, place in a lidded container or ziplock bag with a paper towel.

GRAINS

Boiling

Equipment: saucepan with fitted lid

Also see **www.wholegrainscouncil.org**

If you can cook rice, you can cook any grain. Grains range greatly in ratios of water to grains but all are cooked the same way.

Put dry grain into a saucepan with water or broth and gently simmer until the liquid is absorbed. Never put too much water and then drain away nutrients. It is better to add a little water during cooking.

Depending on the grain, it can take from 15–60 minutes to fully cook. Follow package directions for specific liquid to grain ratio and for yield. For example, brown rice—$2^{1}/_{2}$ cups, for 25–45 minutes will produce 3–4 cups. Quinoa—2 cups, for 12–15 minutes will produce 3 plus cups.

Soaking

Few people seem to do it but cooking time can be lessened if the grains are soaked for several hours. Cook in the same soaking water, adding small amounts if evaporation absorbed too much.

NUTS

Toasted/Roasted

Equipment: baking sheet or toaster oven or heavy-bottom skillet

Spread raw nuts evenly and watch closely as they have a high fat content and can burn suddenly. (The same alert for any seeds like sesame or sunflower.)

It is best to roast at no higher than 170 degrees (about 15–20 minutes) in order to avoid damaging the fat content that can oxidize fat in the bloodstream, producing free radicals. Avoid commercially roasted nuts for this reason.

Store raw nuts in the refrigerator or freezer to prevent rancidity.

BEANS

Boiling

Equipment: saucepan with fitted lid

Although you can use a slow cooker, steam, blanch, or bake, the most used method is simply soaking and boiling. Beans are relied on in many cultures for their protein, fiber, calcium, phosphorus, and iron. Although you can use canned beans, dried beans give the best flavor. Prepare this way:

Cover beans with water and allow to soak overnight or at least 8 hours to be sure they are well-cleaned and allow for better water absorption for more uniform and shortened cooking time.

Drain, rinse very well to rid of dirt and gas causing sugars.

Use fresh water for cooking.

Do not put salt in the water with beans at the beginning as it can toughen the skins of the beans, hinder water absorption, and possibly cause them to split.

Basically, 1 cup of dry navy beans equals 3 cups cooked for 3–4 people.

By the way, peas and lentils do not need to be pre-soaked.

For more charts and cooking instructions see **www.usdrybeans.com**.

"It is the position of the American Dietetic Association that appropriately planned vegetarian diets, including total vegetarian or vegan diets, are healthful, nutritionally adequate, and may provide health benefits in the prevention and treatment of certain diseases. Well-planned vegetarian diets are appropriate for individuals during all stages of the life cycle, including pregnancy, lactation, infancy, childhood, and adolescence, and for athletes."

— Craig WJ, Mangels AR; American Dietetic Association.
J Am Diet Assoc. 2009 Jul;109(7):1266-82.
PMID: 19562864

GOOD THINGS TO KNOW— ABOUT NUTRITION

PROTEIN

YES! There's plenty in plant foods! Know that all plant foods have some protein. Eat a variety and don't worry about getting enough protein. You will get plenty for optimal health without much effort. Athletes have a faster recovery from workouts and sustain higher energy on a plant diet, just ask some Olympians, fighters, and high performance entertainers.

Did you know that animal products have no fiber? Fiber is the roughage we need to have a healthy digestive and elimination system. Only plant foods will do this job.

HOW MUCH IS NEEDED?

53 grams daily according to the USDA, more or less to size and gender.

BEST PLANT SOURCES:

Seitan (wheat gluten as meat substitute) 3 ounces, 31 grams

Tempeh (fermented soybean cake as meat substitute), 1 cup, 41 grams

Lentils (red, green), 1 cup, 18 grams

Beans, (black, kidney, navy, pinto, great Northern, etc.), 1 cup, about 15 grams

Chickpeas (garbanzo beans), 1 cup, 11 grams

Tofu (coagulated soy milk, bean curd), 4 ounces, 11 grams

Soy milk (with fortification, exceeds value of cow's milk), 1 cup, 8 to 11 grams

Quinoa (keen-wah), the highest protein grain, 1 cup, 9 grams

Hemp seeds, 1 ounce, 9 grams

Almonds, raw, $1/4$ cup, 8 grams

Veggie burger (some better than others based on ingredients), 1 patty, 8–22 grams

Pasta, whole grain, 1 cup, 8–10 grams

Peanut butter, 2 tablespoons, 7 grams

Sunflower seeds, ¼ cup, 6 grams

Spinach, 1 cup, 5 grams

Whole-grain bread, 2 slices, 5–8 grams

Brown rice, 1 cup, 5 grams

Tahini (sesame seed paste) and sesame seeds, 2 tablespoons, almost 6 grams

Broccoli, 1 cup, 5 grams

Nutritional yeast (not Brewer's yeast), 1½ tablespoons, 8 grams, a deactivated yeast cultured with a mix of sugarcane and beet molasses. This is perfect protein and rich in B-complex vitamins, although considered a supplement, it is a nutritious ingredient in recipes.

Protein list and amounts from The USDA Nutrient Database for Standard Reference, Release 18, 2005, and manufacturer's information. As also suggested in *Vegan Cooking for Dummies*, Alexandra Jamieson.

IRON

There's plenty in plant foods! Unlike what many might think, there is little difference in iron deficiency issues when comparing vegans and meat-eaters. Iron has a big job in carrying oxygen to the blood and throughout the body. Requirements can vary based on age. Women lose iron during menstruation yet need less after menopause.

Iron in supplement form should only be used if there is a deficiency. A blood test can determine the amount needed and the duration of use with a doctor's recommendation. Some deficiency symptoms can be unusual fatigue, reduced immunity to viruses and disease, pale skin, hair loss, and brittle nails.

HOW MUCH IS NEEDED?

Men, 8 milligrams per day

Women, 18 milligrams per day

After 51 years old, 8 milligrams per day for both sexes

During pregnancy, 27 milligrams per day

According to the National Institutes of Health

Cereals, complete iron fortified, $3/4$ cup, 18 milligrams

Oatmeal, instant, fortified, 11 milligrams

Soybeans, boiled, 1 cup, 8.8 milligrams

Lentils, boiled, 1 cup, 6.6 milligrams

Beans, kidney, boiled, 1 cup, 5.2 milligrams

Black-eyed peas, navy beans, lima beans, boiled, 1 cup, 4.3 milligrams

Tofu, raw, firm, $1/2$ cup, 3.4 milligrams

Spinach, fresh, boiled, $1/2$ cup, 3.2 milligrams

Raisins, $1/2$ cup, 1.6 milligrams

Grits, 1 cup, 1.5 milligrams

Molasses, 1 tablespoon, 0.9 milligrams

Whole-wheat bread, 1 slice, 0.7 milligrams

As suggested in *Vegan Cooking for Dummies*, Alexandra Jamieson.

CALCIUM

Yes! There's plenty in plant foods. We all know that we need calcium for strong bones. But, we also need it for nerve and muscle function, and blood clotting. The dairy marketers imply the only source must be from cow's milk. The truth is that the countries with the highest intake of cow's milk have the highest rates of osteoporosis. Heredity, race, smoking, excessive alcohol, and inactivity (lack of weight-bearing exercise) all play a part in bone health.

Sodium increases loss of calcium—1 gram of salt causes about 5–10 milligrams calcium loss.[*] Adequate vitamin D is essential for optimal absorption of calcium. See vitamin D (pages 29–30).

HOW MUCH IS NEEDED?

1,000 milligrams daily according to the Institute of Medicine and more for those over the age of 50, generally, more or less to age, gender, and size.

[*] Vegetarian Resource Group, **www.vrg.org/nutrition/calcium** for documentation by Reed Mangels, Ph.D; and *The Kind Diet*, Alicia Silverstone, pages 34–43.

Blackstrap molasses, 2 tablespoons, 400 milligrams
Collard greens, cooked, 1 cup, 357 milligrams
Tofu (processed with calcium sulfate), 4 ounces, 200–300
  milligrams (brands differ)
Orange juice, calcium-fortified, 8 ounces, 300 milligrams
Soy or rice milk, calcium-fortified, plain, 8 ounces, 200–300
  milligrams (brands differ)
Turnip greens, cooked, 1 cup, 249 milligrams
Tempeh, 1 cup, 215 milligrams
Kale, cooked, 1 cup, 179 milligrams
Soybeans, cooked, 1 cup, 175 milligrams
Bok choy, cooked, 1 cup, 158 milligrams
Tahini, 2 tablespoons, 128 milligrams
Broccoli, cooked, 1 cup, 94 milligrams
Almonds, ¼ cup, 89 milligrams, or 2 tablespoons almond butter,
  86 milligrams

According to the Vegetarian Resource Group

VITAMIN A

Vegans use plant-derived beta-carotene to create vitamin A in the body. Just as our bodies can make vitamin D through sun exposure, our bodies can make vitamin A from beta-carotene intake. However, most nutritionists do not advise taking beta-carotene in supplement form, as it can interfere with absorption of other nutrients. Vitamin A is important for optimal health, affecting the immune system, cell reproduction, nerve function, and anti-oxidant properties that protect against many diseases.

HOW MUCH IS NEEDED?

Upper limit is 15,000 IU per day according to the National
  Academy of Sciences.

BEST PLANT SOURCES:

Look for foods deep in color. For instance, darker greens have more beta-carotene than light greens, and so on. Get it by eating a variety of dark greens like kale, broccoli, and watercress; colorful fruits and vegetables like tomatoes, red bell peppers, oranges, carrots, sweet potatoes, and many, many others.

VITAMIN D

Not much is naturally present in foods. It is more like a hormone than a vitamin. We need it for calcium absorption, bone health, immune function, Alzheimer's prevention, healthy cell growth, cancer prevention, and as an anti-inflammatory. It can be taken as a supplement, added to foods as "fortified," and absorbed through exposure to the sun.

Vegans should look for supplements labeled D2 (derived from torula yeast, mushrooms, or other plant sources) as it is free of animal sources, unlike D3 (derived from lanolin from sheep's wool). In addition, choose the supplement in pill form or "vegi-caps" since regular gel caps are made from animal bones and skin. However, a D3 for vegans has been created, called Vitashine, in a spray for use on food or in capsule form.

Sunshine helps create vitamin D as it hits our skin and triggers a synthesis. Consider precautions for exposure based on your skin type. Exposure for 5–30 minutes, without sunscreen or no higher than 8 SPF,* two times a week is suggested on average. Use sunscreen after this time for protective measures. There are varying suggestions about exposure, sunscreen, and duration.

HOW MUCH IS NEEDED?

1000 IU to 5000 IU per day is required for optimal function of the many systems in which vitamin D is involved. Note that everyone's ability to synthesize vitamin D in their skin or absorb it from their GI tracts varies greatly. Therefore, it is best to check personal abilities by keeping the blood level between 30 ng/dl and 50 ng/dl, determined with a blood test.

If you have determined your level of D3 and are switching to D2, be aware that it is only about half as potent as D3 and adjust accordingly.

BEST PLANT SOURCES:

Orange juice, fortified with vitamin D, 1 cup, 139–259 IU

* *Becoming Vegan*, Brenda Davis, R.D. and Vesanto Melina, M.S., R.D., page 135.

Cereal, fortified with various amounts, such as Kellogg's All-Bran, 1/2 cup, 131 IU

Soy milk and rice milk, fortified, 1 cup, 297–338 IU (depends on brand)

Tofu, such as Nasoya light firm, one serving 79 grams, 581 IU (depends on brand)

Soy yogurt, plain, one serving container, 161 IU

Mushrooms, white, sliced, 1 cup, 164 IU

According to the National Institutes of Health (NIH)

VITAMIN C

It is everywhere in the plant world. Even the meat-eaters get it from plants! Excess vitamin C (more than 2,000 milligrams per day) may cause kidney stones and diarrhea. Vitamin C solely from food sources is rarely in excess. Everyone thinks of vitamin C for colds, but it is not proven to help once symptoms start. Keeping vitamin C levels up daily is the key. It can also quickly lower blood pressure in stressful situations. Consider eating an orange about an hour before that important interview and stay calmer than anticipated!

More seriously, vitamin C is an important antioxidant and protects against many diseases. It forms collagen to hold cells together and promotes healthy teeth and gums. It helps absorb iron and keeps blood vessels healthy while helping to metabolize protein. It is a big deal!

HOW MUCH IS NEEDED?

90 milligrams per day for men and 75 milligrams for women are recommended, according to National Institutes of Health. Some nutritionists feel 250–1,000 milligrams per day is acceptable to counteract pollution.

BEST PLANT SOURCES:

Papaya, 1 medium, 188 milligrams

Orange, 1 medium, 83 milligrams

Red bell pepper, 1/2 cup cooked, 60 milligrams

Broccoli, 1/2 cup cooked, 58 milligrams

Strawberries, $^1/_2$ cup, 49 milligrams
Brussels sprouts, $^1/_2$ cup cooked, 48 milligrams
Cantaloupe, $^1/_2$ cup, 30 milligrams
Cauliflower, $^1/_2$ cup cooked, 27 milligrams
Kale, $^1/_2$ cup cooked, 26 milligrams
Sweet potato, $^1/_2$ cup cooked, 21 milligrams
Mustard greens, $^1/_2$ cup cooked, 18 milligrams
And many more!

VITAMIN B-12

One of the 8 vitamins, we need B-12 for brain function, the nervous system, the formation of blood, fatty acid synthesis, and energy production. Oddly, B-12 is not made in animals or plants. It comes from bacteria. So how do any human beings get it?

Since few people pull their own carrots out of the soil where B-12 is and eat it or drink water from a stream; and since animals more and more are not putting their noses in the soil while grazing, B-12 must come from foods fortified with it or through supplements. It can be produced very well industrially through bacterial fermentation-synthesis.

HOW MUCH IS NEEDED?

After reading so many opinions on B-12, I needed to seek a confident answer. There is none better than the advice of Dr. Michael Klaper. His conclusion is,

An average of 10 mcg to 25 mcg daily will meet the needs of most people with normal B-12 absorption.

The higher dosages now commonly available allow a single 1000 mcg dose to be taken only once or twice per week. This larger dosage also makes it more likely that older people, those with intestinal diseases, and those with less efficient B-12 absorption can absorb enough B-12 to avoid deficiencies, without resorting to B-12 injections.

1000 mcg 1–2 times a week

If a deficiency, 1000 mcg everyday for 6 weeks, then 1000 mcg, 1–2 times weekly.

Nutritional yeast, Red Star brand, for vegans
Soy milk, fortified
Cereals, fortified
Supplement pills of B-12, regular or sublingual (under the tongue
    version)

OMEGA-3S

In the fat world there are:

Monounsaturated fatty acids—liquid at room temperature like oils of
    olives, peanuts, and avocados.

Polyunsaturated fatty acids—liquid at room temperature, which
    include the essential omega-3 fatty acids, the good fats from
    food, as well as the pro-inflammatory omega-6 fats.

Saturated fatty acids—solid at room temperature; mostly in animal
    products with tropical oils being the only plant source.

Trans fatty acids—solid at room temperature; unsaturated fats
    produced when oils are hydrogenated in a lab to solidify for
    longevity of a product. These are harmful, cell damaging, and
    should be avoided. Use nothing marked "hydrogenated" or
    "partially hydrogenated."

Triglycerides—a chemical form created in the cells when excess
    sugars are eaten in the diet.

We need omega-3s for brainpower and for our hearts to operate. Quite
important! They help prevent disease and balance out the excessive intake of
pro-inflammatory omega-6s that are so huge in the Standard American Diet,
rightly initialed S.A.D.

Many people use fish oils for their omega-3s but fail to consider how con-
taminated they are with high levels of heavy metals, like mercury and lead, and
pollutants from industrial waste. They are considered carcinogenic. And, like
all animal products, it decomposes rather quickly, causing free radicals to form.
Not good. And, guess where the fish get their omega-3s . . . from plants! (The
fish swallow algae cells, which float in the ocean water.) Since omega-3 oils in
"fish oil" (labeled DHA and EPA) really come from algae, we can cut out the
middle fish! Therefore, look for algae derived omega-3s and DHA supplements.

Plant omega-3s are long lasting, unlike fish sources, and come with added gifts of antioxidants that busily sweep away free radicals.

Vegans must pay attention so that omega-6s are eaten in plentiful amounts in soybeans (tofu) and seeds such as sesame (tahini), pumpkin, and sunflower; nuts such as pine nuts and pistachios; olives and oil; and wheat germ.

HOW MUCH IS NEEDED?

Omega-3 balance can be maintained with 1 tablespoon of ground flaxseed per day, 1 teaspoon of flaxseed oil (refrigerated), or vegan algae-based supplements.

BEST PLANT SOURCES:

There are foods that have a good balance of 3s and 6s all in one place—those amazing green leafy vegetables. Seems they are suggested at every turn for every reason. Also, walnuts and hemp seeds contain a good balance.

OILS

There are various views about oils in relation to their place in the diet. Following are some points to consider.

All oils come from plants. See the facing page for more about the three categories of fatty acids: monounsaturated, polyunsaturated, and saturated. And, it might be surprising that all fats are comprised of a mix of all three, only in differing amounts.

Neutral tasting oils, extra virgin olive oil and cold-pressed canola, have the most favorable monounsaturated fatty acids, making them good choices. However, others are fine as well since no plant oil has much saturated fat, except tropical plant oils, such as palm oils, which have very highly saturated fatty acids, 50–80%.

But, be clear: as Dr. Michael Klaper states, all oils are simply liquid fat, making them technically a junk food. There are few nutrients and lots of calories. Oils make you fat and badly affect hormones, possibly contributing to breast lumps and prostate enlargements. They are the "white sugar" of the fat world.

But, if using oil, or starting to back away, there are some valuable points to know. Oils differ and can be quite complicated to sort out. So, briefly, know that the methods used to obtain the oil are significant and also determine heat tolerance.

Type of oils: Distinguish between *refined* and *unrefined* oils. Refined oils are extracted with solvents and they accept higher heat, known as a smoke point, which is good for frying. Unrefined oils are considered better as they are cold-pressed (expeller pressed) with little heat. They have a lower smoke point, good for low to medium-high heat, and are used raw for sauces and salad dressings. Refrigerate after opening to avoid early rancidity. Warning—heating oil above its smoke point produces toxic fumes and free radicals. Not good. See **www.spectrumorganics.com** for more information.

Care of oils: A strong, stale, old smell means it is rancid. Toss out. Oil is destroyed by light (keep in dark glass bottles), heat (keep away from the stove), and air (keep closed). Keep refrigerated unless you have a small bottle that will be used within a couple months.

The more unsaturated oil is, the more likely it is to become rancid. To extend shelf life, some companies pull a fast one, so to speak, and resort to hydrogenation. This is the process that turns oils into margarine so it is solid at room temperature and skyrockets heart disease. Avoid any product that states "partially hydrogenated" on the label, as they are the nasty trans fatty acids. And, you will be surprised how many boxes in your kitchen have this on the ingredient label. Check! Read Marion Nestle's *What to Eat*, for her chapter on "Oils: Fat and More Fat."

Cholesterol: Remember that high cholesterol (high levels of fat in the blood) is mainly found in animal products. Plant sources have little.

HOW MUCH IS NEEDED?

1 tablespoon of any oil = 120 calories

WHAT TO BUY FOR COOKING:

Of course there are no hard dividing lines about where and when to use a specific oil, only suggestions. Never allow any oil to reach the smoke point.

A refined oil has a higher smoke point for higher heat (like corn, vegetable, and refined canola).

Unrefined oil has a lower smoke point for lower heat cooking (sunflower); medium heat for sautéing (safflower, walnut, extra virgin olive oil, sesame, and peanut); high heat (expeller or cold-pressed canola, coconut); for using as a cold dressing (flaxseed, sesame, and extra virgin olive oil).

Coconut oil is unusually high in saturated fat, 90%, unusual for a plant source. It can withstand high heat, remains solid at room temperature, and is resistant to rancidity. Some report that it has properties to compensate for the high saturation (if not hydrogenated) and should not be thought about as bad. However, it is still a fat with the same calories as any other. Certainly, if it is added to the already high fat Standard American Diet (S.A.D.), it is an unfavorable mix.

HOW TO COOK WITHOUT OIL:

If sautéing or frying, use half oil—half broth as a start. Or, use any of these liquids alone.

Bouillon cubes made into broth

Better Than Bouillon vegetable base, purchased in a jar and looks like apple butter (Sometimes, I add a teaspoon or so directly to the skillet and add a few tablespoons of water and stir before adding the food items.)

Purchased or homemade broth

Wines, leftover or mixed with water

Water

Mild teas (perhaps leftover from breakfast)

Bragg Aminos

Fruit juices (lemon, lime, and orange juice work well with greens)

If only concerned about food sticking to the pan, put some oil on a paper towel and rub over the skillet. Usually, food unsticks once it cooks long enough to create a more solid surface, so allow cooking some before trying to move the food. Or, sparingly use one of the nonstick cooking sprays.

SWEETENERS

Cane and beet sugar have little redeeming value except that we really like it! Whatever carbohydrates are in it can be found from better sources for energy and brain function. Basically, it has empty calories. We all think it is rather addictive, and for good reason, as it actually has a drug-like affect in the brain when the tongue tastes it. The brain registers it in much the same way as morphine or heroin![*]

So what to do? Buy the best quality sugar options. There is no need for

---

[*] Dr. Neal Barnard, Physicians Committee for Responsible Medicine (PCRM), in his many books, discusses sugar and also how it relates to diabetes.

super white refined sugar that is filtered through bone char; not vegan! Most commercial white sugar comes from either cane or beet root. I discovered that once I started to taste better sugar options, I experienced a wonderfully rich, deeper taste, and less of a chemical or "too sweet" taste. Buy organic to be sure you have a vegan product.

HOW MUCH IS NEEDED?

In order to avoid many diseases The American Heart Association suggests limiting added sugars to 100 calories or 25 grams for women and 150 calories or 37 grams for men of added sugars per day. Each gram of sugar equals 4 calories. Added sugars mean those in processed foods and in the sugar bowl. Half of a 12-ounce can of soda has 25 grams.

TYPES OF SUGAR PRODUCTS:

Cane sugar : Sometimes labeled as evaporated cane sugar. It is vegan if organic. Most others are filtered with animal bone char.

White sugar : Florida Crystals and Wholesome Sweeteners are widely available brands.

Brown sugar : Made from sugar cane with the molasses left in. Sucanat is the most popular brand; Rapadura is another.

Beet sugar : White vegan sugar, but beets are highly genetically modified (GMO), unless organic. It looks just the same as cane sugar and used in the same ways.

Maple sugar : The end product after boiling away all the water from maple syrup. Sold in blocks or pressed candy. It is twice as sweet as white granulated sugar.

Maple syrup : Obtained from maple tree sap and boiled to a thicker substance. It contains calcium, zinc, and manganese. Grade A, an amber shade, is lighter in flavor, and a Grade B is darker and richer in flavor . . . the one I prefer for pancakes, ice cream sundaes, and most other treats.

Molasses : (Blackstrap) Very dark, strong, rich, and full of calcium, other minerals, and vitamins—some redeeming value in a form of sugar after all. Besides using in baking and barbecue sauce, use instead of coffee in a latte.

Brown rice syrup : Made from brown rice, it has a mellow taste making it perfect for many uses. It is becoming very popular for not allowing blood sugar to plummet.

Barley malt syrup : Made from sprouted barley and is similar to brown rice syrup, but darker and stronger with a malt-like taste. Not as sweet as white sugar.

Agave syrup or nectar : From the agave plant and is sweeter than honey but used in most ways honey would be used in a dish. It is sold in light, dark, and raw styles.

Honey : is not considered a vegan product.

Stevia : A better option to artificial sweeteners, which are mostly coal-tar derivatives. It comes from the tropical stevia plant, has little affect on blood sugar, and is sold in powder and liquid forms. It is 300 times sweeter than sugar, so use just a little!

SOY

A bean! It has great levels of protein and other nutrients and is used in many forms for anyone's diet, but it is especially important to vegans.

HOW MUCH IS NEEDED?

2 to 4 servings a day

Liquid: 8 ounce servings, such as soy milk or miso

Solid: $1/2$ cup, such as edamame, tofu, and tempeh

So, what is too much? The controversy over amounts of soy is uncertain and ongoing. I recommend looking to the latest research on soy to be more accurate. You will find more or less amounts as good or bad in relation to blood pressure, cholesterol, breast or prostate cancer, sperm count levels, Alzheimer's, and other health issues.

However, there are a few points to consider when choosing the amount of soy intake. Many of the soy products are highly processed, just like the non-vegan similar items. So, commonsense would cause us to consider using them as transition foods in order to have similar for similar, such as, a hot dog for a hot dog. High sodium and tons of preservatives are also a concern. At the same time, start to add whole foods to your diet, like fresh salads, soups, beans and grains, nuts and seeds. Then, use less of the soy processed items. See more nutritional facts about soy in The Other Proteins (pages 104–113).

BEST SOURCES:

Most obtain it from soy milk but also as edamame, which are soybeans; miso, a soybean seasoning; veggie burgers and hot dogs, soy sauce, and even dairy-like products such as sour cream, cream cheese, yogurt, and ice cream.

Most soybeans in the U.S. are genetically modified because such high levels of pesticides are used on them. It is best to use organic products when possible.

EGGS

We have to face it. There is no way to make anything that requires more than two eggs, such as items like meringue or an angel food cake. However, these are seldom-missed items. I can live well without them. But, because of the demand for vegan products, there will be answers coming for almost everything.

For baking, there are sometimes confusing ingredient adjustments you can make by adding vinegar or water and then more or less flour or baking soda. A Web search can produce many listings for a one egg substitute—mashed potatoes, pumpkin, puréed prunes, or tofu. I honestly see no point. Not all of them work equally for any recipe and flavor profiles can be compromised in some cases. If I want to make muffins, I find a great vegan muffin recipe, or a vegan cake recipe to take the guesswork out. The world has caught up with vegan baking.

Or better yet, get Fran Costigan's *More Great Good Dairy-Free Desserts Naturally* and simply bake from her book. She has already developed perfectly moist, perfectly sweetened dessert recipes ready to make.

There are times to recreate the work an egg does, like in Favorite and Fast Pancakes (page 45). In these cases, use a 1 1/2 teaspoons of starch powder* mixed with 2 tablespoons water to make a thickened substance and add along with the wet ingredients.

For dishes with a more visible egg-like requirement, use crumbled firm tofu to make Ella's Scrambled "Eggs" with Potatoes and Onions (page 44) or Diner Egg and Olive Salad Sandwich (page 126).

Commercial egg production is against all things vegan. The excessive cruelty to the chickens is well documented by Karen Davis, whose exhaustive work reveals the truth in her book, *Poisoned Chickens, Poisoned Eggs*.

---

* Ener-G Egg Replacer

Good Things

TO EAT

RECIPES AND TIPS

BREAKFAST POWER

Creamy Anytime Oats

From Fran Costigan's *More Great Good Dairy-Free Desserts Naturally*

Serves 1

I never thought something as simple as soaking oatmeal overnight with soy milk in a cereal bowl, ready to go in the morning, would be exciting. It is!

Rolled oats .... $^1/_3$ cup
Nondairy milk (soy, almond, etc.) .... $^1/_2$ cup
Nuts of choice (almonds, walnuts, etc.) .... **2** tablespoons, chopped
Fresh or dried fruit or berries .... **2** tablespoons, or to taste
Soy yogurt

Combine oats and nondairy milk in a small container and cover. Refrigerate overnight or 8–24 hours to soften oats. (The longer they soak, the creamier the oats will be.) Top with nuts, fruits, and soy yogurt, if desired.

Original Granola with Banana Milk

I love the idea of using the calcium and iron-rich blackstrap molasses as a sweetener and also love the flavor so much. When traveling, this is a must to carry for the hotel room breakfast along with individual soy milks.

GRANOLA

Makes 8 cups

Grain flakes (a mix of oats, spelt, barley, and kamut or others)	4 cups
Sunflower seeds	1 cup
Walnuts	1 1/2 cups, chopped
Cinnamon	1 1/2 teaspoons
Ground ginger	1 1/2 teaspoons
Safflower, peanut, or vegetable oil	1/4 cup
Blackstrap molasses	1/3 cup
Water	1/3 cup
Wheat germ	1/2 cup
Sesame seeds	1/4 cup
Flax seeds, ground (use spice grinder, if needed)	1/4 cup

In a wok or very large skillet, combine grain flakes, sunflower seeds, walnuts, cinnamon, and ginger. Mix oil, molasses, and water; pour over dry mixture. Stir well over medium heat. When mixture is dryer and heated through, add wheat germ, sesame and flax seeds. Continue stirring from the bottom until lightly toasted. Allow it to cool completely. Stewed prunes or dried fruit are a nice addition when serving.

BANANA MILK

Makes 2 cups

Ice cold water	**2** cups
Bananas	**2**, peeled and sliced
Vanilla	**1**$^1/_2$ teaspoons
Maple syrup	**1** tablespoon

Briefly blend all ingredients in a blender. Make just what you will use immediately in one meal as it can discolor. For one serving, make a quarter to half of the recipe above based on personal preference.

Chocolate-Stuffed French Toast with Rice Krispies

Serves 4

I know! Decadent! Chef Josef Huber at the Amway Grand Plaza Hotel in Grand Rapids, MI, offered a version of this for *Great Chefs Cook Vegan* using homemade bread and a fruit compote. This is a faster version.

DIPPING BATTER

Soy milk, vanilla	**1**$^1/_2$ cups
Orange juice, freshly squeezed	$^2/_3$ cup
Cinnamon	**1** teaspoon
Maple syrup	**3** tablespoons
Egg replacer (Ener-G)	**1** tablespoon

For a grown-up addition, add 2 tablespoons Grand Marnier liqueur

Whisk together ingredients and pour into a pan large enough for a sandwich.

CHOCOLATE-STUFFED FRENCH TOAST

Vegan chocolate chips .... **8**-ounce bag (check ingredients
for no milk products)
Whole-grain bread (Ezekiel 4:9
and Food for Life) .... **8** slices
Rice Krispies .... **2²/₃** cups
Toppings: sliced bananas (or other fruit), pure maple syrup, a dusting of
vegan powered sugar, or vegan margarine, if desired

Melt chocolate chips in the microwave at 10 second intervals, stirring each time, or slowly in a heavy saucepan over very low heat. Spread the chocolate on 4 slices of bread and place the other bread slices on top. Put the Rice Krispies in a bowl and set beside the batter pan. Place one sandwich into the Dipping Batter and soak for 20 seconds turning over halfway through. Coat the bread slices with Rice Krispies immediately.

Heat a griddle or skillet over medium heat and coat with vegetable spray. Place the sandwiches on the griddle and cook until the bottom turns golden brown; flip and brown the other side. Serve with toppings of choice.

Ella's Scrambled "Eggs" with Potatoes and Onions

Inspired from Ella Nemcova's *Regal Vegan Recipe* **www.regalvegan.com.**

Serves 1

Onion powder	$1/2$ teaspoon
Turmeric	$1/8$ teaspoon
Chipotle powder or chili powder or paprika	$1/8$ teaspoon
Celery salt	$1/2$ teaspoon
Nutritional yeast	1 teaspoon
Potato	1 small, peeled and cut into chunks
Tamari or soy sauce	1 tablespoon
Water	1 cup
Canola or extra virgin olive oil	1 teaspoon
Onion	1 small, chopped
Tofu, firm	$1/4$ pound or $1/2$ tub
Spinach, fresh	2 handfuls

Mix onion powder, turmeric, chipotle powder, celery salt, and nutritional yeast together in a small bowl and set aside.

Boil potato in salted water to fork tender. In a small bowl, mix the tamari with water and set aside.

Heat oil in a small frying pan over medium heat. Add onion and sauté until tender. Sprinkle spice mixture around the pan and stir to coat onion. Crumble in tofu, add liquid mixture, and stir. Add potato and spinach and stir mixture until spinach leaves wilt. Serve with a side of multigrain toast and spicy chili sauce, if desired.

Favorite and Fast Pancakes

Makes about 6 (4-inch) pancakes

I often do not want to make anything that requires mixing several dry ingredients like flour, baking soda, baking powder, and so on. It is not hard and does not take much time, but somehow it is the idea of it. A premix already does that, so sometimes I start at a better place in the process.

Bisquick	$1/2$ cup
Rolled oats, quick	$1/2$ cup
Soy milk* or other alternative	$3/4$ to 1 cup
Egg replacer (Ener-G)	$1 1/2$ teaspoons powder mixed with 2 tablespoons warm water
Walnuts or sliced almonds	$1/4$ cup, chopped, optional
Cinnamon	$1/4$ teaspoon, optional
Blueberries or strawberries, frozen or fresh, optional	
Pure maple syrup, grade B, optional	
Vegan margarine, optional	

Heat a skillet (cast iron works well for this) or griddle to medium high while making the batter, adding some vegetable oil just to coat. In a bowl, combine all the ingredients except fruit, syrup, and margarine, if using. Add more milk for thinner pancakes. Test a drop of water in the skillet for a sizzle and then pour $1/4$ cup batter for 1 pancake. Turn over when bubbles appear on the top and edges seem puffy and well rounded. You can either drop pieces of fruit into the pancake before flipping or serve as a topping on the cooked pancakes.

Note: Bisquick has partially hydrogenated oil as an ingredient. If this is an issue, substitute with many recipes where all dry ingredients are assembled.

*I prefer Westsoy Plus Vanilla but any milk alternative is fine.

DRINKS FOR ALL REASONS

Orange Creamsicle Frosty Drink

Serves 2

I loved Creamsicles as a kid, way before the vegan years! It is nice to get the taste back in some form. Childhood has such good taste memories.

Oranges..2 medium
Ice cream, vanilla soy or rice......................1 cup, or to taste

Place two glasses or mugs in the freezer. Cut the rind off the oranges, trying to cut exactly between the white and orange areas. It is best to hold the orange in one hand and seesaw cut from the top, spiraling around the orange until reaching the bottom. Once all the peel is gone, hold the same way and cut along a membrane of an orange section into the center of the orange, being careful not to cut past the center. Cut along the side of each membrane until all sections fall away.

Blend ingredients in the blender until just smooth, preserving the thickness.

Frozen Fruit and Green Smoothie

Serves 1 (large mug) or 2 (8-ounce cups)

Once you make this, you will instantly see how to vary which fruit or green you use and in what amounts to suit your taste. But, start here and then follow your creative spirit. Only the fruit flavors come through.

Banana, frozen	$^1/_2$ large, sliced into half-inch pieces
Blueberries, frozen	$^1/_2$ to 1 cup
Soy milk, vanilla* (I prefer Westsoy Plus Vanilla)	1 cup
Spinach, fresh	2 cups, packed (can be optional for a fruit only smoothie)

*Also consider vanilla rice milk, almond milk, apple juice, orange juice, or water.

Place the ingredients into a blender in the order given (important), pushing down hard on the spinach. Run the blender on high, turning off and pushing spinach into mix, if needed. Notice if you should add a tad more liquid because of your blender's ability. Once the spinach disappears into the mix, blend for about 10 seconds only.

If you happen to have a fluid-filled freezer mug, pour into that and eat with a spoon if the amount of liquid is not too much. It should be almost like soft frozen custard. Otherwise, drink as a thick shake.

Note: The fluid-filled plastic mugs for freezing can be found at kitchen shops and some national drug stores in the summer. But, of course, any glass or mug will do.

Gene Baur's Green Smoothie

Serves 3–4

It seems every seriously health-conscious person has their own version of a green smoothie. Gene is in constant motion and needs intense nutrition as head of the Farm Sanctuary, animal rescue farms in New York and California.

So, this is license to go forth and use this recipe as a guide and then design one with your name on it.

Nondairy milk	**2** cups
Banana	**1**
Blueberries, frozen	**1/4** cup
Kale	**2** large leaves
Spinach	**1/2** cup, or more
Cucumber, chunks	**1/2** cup, optional
Flax seeds or hemp seeds or	
chia seeds, ground	**1 1/2** teaspoons
Date, pitted	**1**
Ice, crushed, optional	

Blend all ingredients until smooth. If you wish it to be thicker, add more fruit or seeds. For thinner, add more milk or water.

Note: Do not confuse smoothies with juiced drinks. Juicing requires a juicing machine that extracts the juice and leaves the pulp. Smoothies can be made in a regular blender and the food items keep all their fiber. However, some raw vegetables, like carrots and beets, cannot be blended well unless softened a bit by boiling, thus only a juicing machine will do for raw vegetable juicing. If buying a machine, be willing to invest in a good one or the produce bill will be higher to yield the same amount of juice extraction.

Slushie

Serves 4

Perhaps this brings memories of childhood. Updated now, just combine the juice flavor you want, sweetener, and a lot of ice in a blender. Even then it was vegan!

Pomegranate juice or cranberry,	
grape, cherry, mango, etc.	**1** cup
Maple syrup, brown rice syrup, or Stevia	**4** teaspoons, or to taste
Ice, crushed	**3** cups

Place all ingredients in a blender and blend until desired consistency.

Superhero Smoothie

Serves 1

It is incredible to see grade-schoolers in Harlem drinking this smoothie and loving it at family nutrition night sponsored by the New York Coalition of Healthy School Food and headed by Amie Hamlin.

Pineapple juice, pure	1 cup
Kale	2 leaves, stems removed
Ice cubes	4 to 5
Bananas, frozen	2

Place juice, kale, and ice cubes in the blender and process until greens are pulverized. Cut banana into chucks, add to the mixture, and blend until smooth. If you have a high-speed blender such as Blendtec or Vita-Mix, the ice cubes might not be needed.

Instead-of-Soda Soda

Serves 1

Make your own soda and escape the bad aspects of purchased ones. One can actually home-brew colas and ginger ales with recipes online. However, I am more of an open-the-refrigerator-and-pour person. These two recipes are almost that.

SODA NUMBER 1

Drop of culinary oil	1 to 2 drops*
Sparkling water	8 to 16 ounces
Ice	

Add culinary oil to a glass of sparkling water, stir, and add ice.

If you must have sweetener, add Stevia or equal parts of evaporated cane juice sugar and water heated well and cooled which makes sugar syrup. Try to use a tiny bit, no more than half a teaspoon per drink. That surely beats the 8–16 teaspoons of refined sugar in one store-bought soda!

Consider using a carbonated water marked sparkling water or seltzer. Although club soda is similar, it has added sodium and some potassium bicarbonate and potassium sulfate, which dulls the sharp effects of effervescence.

*LorAnn Oils online, and in baking supply stores, sells great inexpensive, natural, water-soluble oils for culinary uses. Use only a drop as they are super strong. Choose the oils for their natural aspects. "Flavors" have artificial aspects. I like lemon and lime together to make a Sprite-like soda, tangerine, ginger, celery seed, and even cola.

More commonly, and an easy request at restaurants, is to combine 50/50 . . .

Sparkling water
Juice (cranberry, orange juice, pomegranate, pineapple, etc.)
Ice

Alicia's Warm Spicy Wine
Glogg (Nordic) or Gluhwein (German)
Serves 10–12

Alicia Silverstone brings her talents of cooking to us as well as her great acting ability. Her book, *The Kind Diet,* is a must for the vegan bookshelf.

Red wine, dry, sulfate-free organic	**1** bottle
Madeira, sweet red wine, or Port	**1** cup
Orange juice, freshly-squeezed	**1** cup, optional
Maple syrup, pure	**¹/₄** to **¹/₂** cup
Cardamom pods	**5** whole, cracked, optional
Cloves	**2** whole
Cinnamon stick	**1**
Orange (fresh or dried)	**2** slices, optional

Combine all the ingredients in a large stainless steel saucepan, heating very slowly over very low heat. DO NOT BOIL. Strain in a mesh strainer and serve immediately, or turn off heat and allow to rest for several hours or overnight. Then strain and gently reheat.

Reprinted from: *The Kind Diet* by Alicia Silverstone. Copyright © 2009 by Alicia Silverstone. Permission granted by Rodale, Inc. Emmaus, PA 18098.

Hot Blackstrap Molasses Drink

Serves 1

Blackstrap is a sweetener that is packed with good things, like minerals such as iron and calcium. For a fast way to see nutrient breakdowns of this and many foods, go to **www.whfoods.com** and type the food into the search box.

Hot water or soy milk	**1** cup
Blackstrap molasses,	
organic and unsulphured*	**1** tablespoon, or to taste
Soy creamer, optional	

Simply heat the liquid as you wish. Dip a tablespoon into the hot drink before filling with the molasses so it slips easily off the spoon. Stir. Add creamer, if using.

*Unsulphured molasses is free of processing chemicals and has a cleaner taste.

Hot Chocolate

Serves 1

I should probably just heat chocolate syrup and call it hot chocolate. I love strong chocolate. Growing up not far from Hershey, PA, I had some early notions about chocolate.

Cocoa powder	**3** tablespoons
Sugar, evaporated cane juice	**1** teaspoon
Sea salt	smallest possible pinch
Vanilla soy milk (I prefer Westsoy	
Plus Vanilla)	**1** cup

In a saucepan, combine the cocoa powder, sugar, and sea salt. Over medium heat, add about a quarter of the soy milk and whisk while the mixture heats and to coax the dry ingredients into the milk. Just before boiling, add the rest of the soy milk. Continue whisking to help form a nice foam on the top. Do not boil.

THE ANATOMY OF A SALAD

Salad? Boring? Have you ever thought that you can make a different one every day of your life? Pick from 1, 2, 3, 4, and 5. You never need to make the same one twice!

1. GREEN IT!

Choose a green, the darker the green the better the nutrients.

2. DEFINE IT!

Choose a main item like beans, pasta, grains, or lentils. In addition, consider tofu or tempeh.

3. EMBELLISH IT!

Turn up the nutrients with a variety of vegetables or fruits or both.

4. GARNISH IT!

Add crunch and flavor—nuts, seeds, herbs, olives, garlic, dried fruit.

5. DRESS IT!

Creamy or vinaigrette, fresh fruit juice, fat-free, or a choice of oil.

BLENDED SALADS

"Blended salads are very good. It is not the same as juicing, but if you are looking for good nutrition and you want another way to eat greens, blend your salad ingredients. Dark green leafy vegetables are the most important for all of us to eat because they boost the immune system and have anti-cancer properties." Caryn Hartglass, **www.responsiblelivingandeating.com.**

THE CREATIVE WORLD OF DRESSINGS

Dressings are made in a flash! Save money, and up the nutrition. Even make some fat-free, if desired. Here are some starters.

I discovered dressings taste different alone. So, taste your salad dressings on a green leaf as you make them and adjust to personal taste, especially for salt, vinegar, and oil proportions.

Vinaigrettes

RICE VINEGAR

Drizzle

This is a very mild vinegar that can be used alone or added to any of your favorite ingredients for dressings that preserve their flavors.

ITALIAN VINAIGRETTE

Makes 1 cup

1 cup olive oil; **2** tablespoons red wine vinegar; **2** small cloves garlic, minced; **1** teaspoon each of dry mustard, tarragon, marjoram; and **¼** teaspoon each of salt and pepper, or to taste. Shake in a lidded jar. Set aside to blend flavors and soften herbs.

BALSAMIC VINAIGRETTE

Makes ½ cup

Whisk **3** tablespoons balsamic vinegar; **2** tablespoons any prepared mustard; **1** tablespoon agave nectar or maple syrup; and a smidge of water. Shake. This "Beam Me Up, Scottie Dressing" is from is from *The Engine 2 Diet* by Rip Esselstyn and Austin firefighter, Scottie Waters.

Creamy

Use many creamy dressings as a sandwich or wrap spread as well.

CREAMY MUSTARD VINAIGRETTE

Makes 3/4 cup

2 tablespoons each red wine vinegar, prepared mustard, and minced onion (or **1** shallot); **1** tablespoon soy creamer, optional; **1/4** teaspoon sea salt; and **1/3** cup oil. Combine all ingredients while slowly whisking in oil.

"SEA CZAR" DRESSING

Makes 3/4 cup

1/2 cup vegan mayonnaise; **3** tablespoons extra virgin olive oil; **1** tablespoon each of lemon juice and water; **1/2** teaspoon each of prepared mustard, crushed garlic, and dulse flakes (add afterward if using a blender); **1** teaspoon white miso; and a pinch of salt. Whisk or blend in a blender.

From Chef Ken Bergeron, *Professional Vegetarian Cooking*

CASHEW DILL DRESSING

Makes 1 cup

Blend **1/2** cup raw cashews to a powder; add **3/4** cup water; **1/4** teaspoon garlic powder; and **1/2** teaspoon each of dry mustard, dried dill weed, and dried basil and blend until very smooth, adding more water for consistency.

SWEET SPICY MUSTARD DRESSING

Makes 2 cups

Cream in a blender, **1** package silken tofu; **1/2** cup each of prepared mustard and pure maple syrup; **2** tablespoons lemon juice; **1/2** teaspoon sea salt, and **1/4** teaspoon cayenne pepper. This is also a super sandwich spread.

From Chef Del Sroufe of The Wellness Forum

RANCH DRESSING

Makes 1 1/2 cups

1 cup mayonnaise; **1/4** cup soy milk or **1/4** cup soy sour cream; **1** tablespoon apple cider vinegar; **1** teaspoon each of garlic powder and onion powder; **1** teaspoon dried parsley (or **2** teaspoons fresh); **1/2** teaspoon dried dill; and **1/4** teaspoon each of sea salt and pepper. Whisk.

TOSSED IS NOT THE ONLY SALAD

These salads are super easy to "toss" together even though they are not really tossed salads as we think of them. Use each recipe as a guide to your own recipes.

"Our Hen House" Bowl

From Our Hen House, www.ourhenhouse.org, and founders Jasmin Singer and Mariann Sullivan.

Who needs a recipe? Use your best judgment and adapt to your appetite as to amounts.

Start with a big bowl.

Put in a layer of a grain first. They like quinoa—red or cream colored or a mix of both.

Layer next with a chopped green (spinach, arugula, others), or their favorite, kale.

Followed by a good protein, any beans, but ideally black beans, or steamed firm tofu. *

Then top with a dressing. They usually drizzle tahini with "more than a little" nutritional yeast.

Note: Most any of the dressings in The Creative World of Dressings (pages 54–55) can be used with this salad.

---

*Steam firm or extra firm tofu for this recipe using the stovetop or microwave. On the stovetop, use a steamer basket in a saucepan with boiling water below the basket and a tight lid for 5–7 minutes. If no basket is on hand, place tofu in a sturdy bowl that will set in the bottom of the saucepan with boiling water below the rim of the bowl. In the microwave, cover a plate of tofu with a damp towel and heat for about $2^1/_2$ minutes.

Baby Zucchini and Avocado Tartar

Serves 4

Chef Matthew Kenney shares this simple, creative, and flavor-packed salad. See all of his Raw cookbook series at **www.gibbs-smith.com.**

Avocado	**2**, finely diced
Zucchini, baby	**4** to **5**, finely diced
Lemon juice	**2** tablespoons
Olive oil	**1** tablespoon
Basil, finely minced	**2** tablespoons
Chives, minced	**1** tablespoon, optional
Salt	**2** teaspoons, or to taste
Ground pepper	to taste

Toss all ingredients until well combined. Top with pepper, if desired.

Edamame Combo Salad

Serves 4

Why do I feel so clever saying the word edamame (ed-a-MAH-may)? It is like I know something special. Edamame are young green soybeans and a great source of protein, 11 grams in a half-cup. Home Economist Jane Belt offered this simple recipe and suggests using leftovers on a layer of arugula.

Edemame, frozen .... **1** (10-ounce) bag, thawed
Corn, frozen .... **1 1/2** cups, thawed
Red onion .... **1** small, chopped
Carrot .... **1** medium, grated

Combine all ingredients in a bowl and set aside.

DRESSING

Lemon .... **1**, juiced and zested
Lime .... **1**, juiced
Olive oil or water .... **2 1/2** tablespoons
Rice vinegar .... **2** tablespoons

Place dressing ingredients in a jar, shake, and pour over salad mixture then chill. Allowing the salad to set for a few hours adds to the flavor.

Variation: Add a tablespoon of toasted sesame oil for extra flavor.

Arugula Watermelon Salad

This is my very favorite salad. The brilliant Chef Gabriel Kreuther at The Modern in the MOMA, New York City, inspired me to make a fast version of his watermelon salad. His had watermelon, tomatoes, toasted pistachios, and some reduced balsamic vinegar.

This one is simply placing a few ingredients on a plate. Amounts are up to you. The strong taste of the arugula against the refreshing cool crunch of the watermelon and the rich depth of the walnuts topped with the tart mustard dressing is truly something.

Arugula
Watermelon cubes
Walnuts (toasted, if desired)
Dressing of prepared mustard, water, salt, and pepper shaken in a jar.

THE ANATOMY OF A SOUP

In 5 simple steps, you've got soup—clear or creamy, hot or cold, a starter or a meal in itself.

1. STOCK IT!

Create your own broth from veggies, miso, vegetable bouillon cubes or powder, or ready-made soup stock.

2. MIREPOIX IT!

Carrots, celery, and onions form the "trinity" of most classic soups—what the French call *mirepoix*. (Formula: 25% carrots, 25% celery, 50% onions,)

3. DEFINE IT!

Give your soup its own identity with beans, veggies, pasta, rice, or tofu.

4. FLAVOR IT!

Add distinction with herbs, spices, greens, tomatoes, or garnishes like vegan cheese and seasoned croutons.

5. CREAM IT . . . OR NOT!

Give your soup extra heartiness by adding a "cream" made from soy milk, tofu, cashews, or other nuts. See Red Lentil Vegetable Soup (page 62) for instructions that can be used when making any soup.

Chef's Vegetable Broth

Yields about 3³/₄ quarts. Eat now, freeze some for future soups, and use for oil-free sautéing.

It is important to have vegetable broth on hand at all times.

Executive Chef Jason Cunningham, of the Washington Duke Inn in Durham, NC, gave me a refined recipe for broth for *Great Chefs Cook Vegan* that brought rave reviews from readers. I asked for a shorter version for this book and he was happy to offer this one, but encourages cooks to also give the other one a try, even if more ingredients.

Olive oil	¹/₄ cup
Onions	**3** medium, coarsely chopped
Celery	**3** stalks, coarsely chopped
Carrots	**2** large, chopped
Leek	**1** medium, white parts, sliced in half, chopped
Salt	**2** teaspoons
Pepper	pinch
White wine, dry	¹/₄ cup, optional
Garlic	**1** whole bulb, halved, crushed
Bay leaf	**1** large or 2 small
Water	**4** quarts

Heat an empty large pot over medium heat; add olive oil and swirl to coat. Add vegetables and salt and pepper, cover, and cook for 3 minutes. Stir well and add wine, if using, and continue cooking 10 minutes more or until vegetables are tender. Add garlic, bay leaf, and water. Cook for 45 minutes. Strain the broth through a mesh sieve.* The broth will last for a week in the refrigerator or 3 months in the freezer.

Variation: This can be considered a vegan "chicken" soup without the bad stuff. Chicken-flavored seitan can be added along with some corn for the vegan version of chicken corn soup. Sip for those flu days.

*I like to put the leftover cooked vegetables in the blender with a bit of broth, water, or even soy milk and have a bowl of creamy soup.

Red Lentil Vegetable Soup with Nut Cream
Serves 6

This is my favorite go-to soup. It is classic in preparation, and once the base of the mirepoix and broth is done, you can then make the soup in any direction by choosing another bean or lentil, or by choosing other vegetables.

The nuts and lentils make this a protein and vitamin-packed soup. Better than chicken soup for those "chicken soup times."

Cashews, raw	$^1/_2$ cup
Water	8 cups
Vegetable bouillon (Rapunzel with Herbs and Sea Salt is one option)	3 cubes
Red lentils	1 cup
Bay leaf	1 or 2
Carrots	4 medium, peeled, sliced
Celery	4 stalks, cut in half lengthwise, sliced
Onion	1 large, medium diced
Potatoes, white or sweet, $^1/_2$-inch cubes*	2 cups
Corn, fresh or frozen	1 cup, optional

Note: All measures can be loosely followed, use more or less to taste.

*When using sweet potatoes, it is best to use raw peanuts instead of cashews. They just go together better and is more like a soup you might have in Africa.

Add cashews to a blender, cover with hot tap water to about a $^1/_2$ inch above the nuts and allow to soak while making the soup. Do not blend yet.

In a large saucepan, add water and bouillon cubes and bring to a boil. Place lentils in a sieve and run cool water to rinse and then add to pot. Allow water to boil again, stirring lentils briefly. Add the bay leaf, carrots, celery, onion, potatoes, and corn, if using. Turn heat to soft boil, uncovered, and cook until tender, about 20 minutes. Remove bay leaf.

Turn blender on high and blend cashews long enough to be completely creamy and super smooth. If too thick, add a bit more water. Add to soup as a last step, creating a hearty base. If not using nuts for some reason, blend 2 ladles of soup instead to create a more sturdy broth to finish.

Potato Parsley Soup (or Bisque)

Adapted from John Robbins' *May All Be Fed*

Serves 6

John Robbins' writings are so inspiring. See his book, *Diet for a New America*. I changed the title from bisque to soup because the bites of soft potato are so good in this. The cashew cream broth still makes it seem like a bisque, but with solid pieces.

Cashews, raw	**1** cup
Vegetable broth or bouillon	**5** cups, divided
Red potatoes	**1** pound, peeled or unpeeled if organic, ¹/₂ inch cubes*
Leeks	**2** medium, chopped
Parsley, fresh, finely chopped	**1** cup
Lemon juice	**1** teaspoon
Sea salt	**1** teaspoon
Pepper	¹/₄ teaspoon

*Although the photo shows unpeeled potatoes for a rustic soup, peeled produces a creamier feel to the soup.

In a blender, blend cashews and 2 cups broth until completely creamy.

In a large pot, combine potatoes, leeks, and remaining broth and bring to a simmer over medium heat. Cover and boil until potatoes are tender, about 10–15 minutes. Add water, if needed. Stir in the cashew mixture, parsley, lemon juice, salt, and pepper. Reduce heat and simmer, stirring often until thickened, about 2 minutes. If desired, transfer some or all of the soup in batches to a blender and process until smooth.

Fast Horseradish Tomato Soup

Serves 2

Tomato soup is a staple of growing up in America. Patti Breitman, a passionate vegan in California, makes life as simple as possible with recipes in her books that are very doable. This is one that I love, but I took the liberty of adding the soy milk for a hot cream soup. Leave it out and eat it cold to be more like Patti.

Tomatoes, whole	1 (28-ounce) BHA-free can or 5 ripe, chopped and seeded
Horseradish	1 teaspoon, or to taste
Onion, sweet	1 small, diced
Lemon juice	1 teaspoon

Pepper	to taste
Soy milk (plain or sweetened)	$\frac{1}{2}$ cup
Whole-grain bread	2 slices
Vegan margarine	

Combine all ingredients in a blender except bread and margarine. Toast bread, spread lightly with margarine, cut diagonally, and add to soup bowl.

Bobbi and Tom's Black Bean Chili with Chipotle Skillet Cornbread

Serves 6–8

A best friend from high school, Bobbi, and her husband, Tom Boock, who owns a restaurant, like to make this oh-so-easy chili when they come home very tired and need to throw something together. Of course, cornbread is a natural with any kind of chili, so I asked Robin Robertson if I could borrow this recipe from *Vegan Planet*, just one of her many helpful books.

Onion	1 medium, coarsely chopped
Green bell pepper	1, diced
Garlic	1 clove, sliced

Water	1/2 cup
Black beans	2 (15.5-ounce) BHA-free cans
Tomatoes, crushed	1 (28-ounce) BHA-free can
Corn	1 (15-ounce) BHA-free can
Chili powder	1 teaspoon
Brown sugar	1 teaspoon, optional
Salt	1/2 teaspoon
Pepper	1/4 teaspoon

Place onion, bell pepper, and garlic in a large saucepan, add water and heat to soften. Add the beans, tomatoes, and corn and simmer just to warm. Add chili powder, brown sugar, salt, and pepper. Simmer a few minutes more.

CHIPOTLE SKILLET CORNBREAD

Yellow cornmeal	1 1/4 cups
Flour, unbleached	1 cup
Salt	1 1/2 teaspoons
Soy milk	1 cup
Maple syrup, pure	3 tablespoons
Corn oil	1/4 cup
Corn (fresh, canned, or frozen)	1 cup
Chipotle chiles in adobo sauce, finely chopped	2 tablespoons

Preheat oven to 400 degrees.

In a large bowl, combine the dry ingredients and set aside. In a medium bowl, combine the liquid ingredients, corn, and chiles and set aside. Heat a well-oiled cast iron skillet over medium heat until hot. While the skillet is heating, add the wet ingredients to the dry and mix well with a few quick strokes. Transfer the batter to the hot skillet and bake on the center of the oven rack until golden brown and a toothpick inserted in the center comes out clean, 25–30 minutes.

USES FOR POWERFUL KALE

Nothing can be all things to all people but kale comes close!

    1 cup = 6 grams of protein
    1 cup = 36 calories
    1 cup = way more than needed in a day of vitamins K and A and
        almost a day's supply of vitamin C! It is also full of iron,
        calcium, and fiber.

HEALTH HIGHS

    Antioxidant and anti-inflammatory
    Anti-cancer, especially bladder, breast, colon, ovary, and prostate
    Cholesterol lowering
    Tons of fiber
    Aids detoxification
    Eat around 2 cups 2–3 times a week or more for the greatest
        benefits.
There are several kinds of kale, but the two most widely available are:
    Curly—ruffled leaves and fibrous stems, soft dark green
    Dinosaur—also known as Tuscan kale or Lacinato kale, dark green
    You can substitute with kale's good cousins—collard greens, Swiss
        chard, mustard greens, broccoli, and cabbage.

Steamed Kale with Garlic and Soy Sauce
(Or how to cook any greens)
Yield 2 cups

I did not know that when I made this recipe from Jennifer Raymond's *Fat-Free & Easy* that it was to become a template for preparing any greens. It is also a way to cook many vegetables. Low calorie, protein, calcium, and even beta-carotene!

Kale	6 to 8 cups, chopped
Water	1/2 cup
Garlic	2 cloves, sliced or minced

Soy sauce or Bragg Liquid Aminos
or pinch of sea salt .... **2** to 3 teaspoons

Rinse the kale. Remove the stems by squeezing the stem at the cut end while holding tight and stripping the leaf forward to the tip in one big swoop. Tear or cut leaves in an inch or larger pieces.

Heat water in a skillet or large pot. Add garlic, soy sauce, and then the greens. Cover and cook over medium heat for 3–5 minutes. With tongs, toss occasionally, adding more water, if needed. Most of the water should evaporate.

Victoria's Incredible Kale Salad
Serves 2–4 (depending if it is a dinner or a side salad)

This could become your favorite classic salad. The simplicity of it is misleading. It is the prep technique that is important for the great flavor. Thanks, Victoria Moran.*

Kale.. **1** bunch
Dressing: Extra virgin olive oil, apple cider vinegar, pink Himalayan salt
 (if unavailable, use sea salt)
Bell pepper, red or yellow .... **1**, chopped

Red onion	$^1/_2$ medium, finely chopped
Black olives, sliced	$^1/_3$ cup
Tomato	1, chopped

To remove the stems from the kale, fold the leaf in half along the stem and run a knife along the spine cutting through the leaf of both sides at the same time. Pile and roll kale leaves and chop to bite-size pieces.

Dressing: Make dressing by putting oil and vinegar, a 3:1 ratio of oil to vinegar, into a jar, add salt to taste, and shake well.

Add dressing to kale and massage the leaves with your fingers for at least 5 minutes. Have fun. Make it a zen moment! For best results, let set for 1 hour to further soften the leaves and absorb flavor of dressing. Add other vegetables, toss, and serve.

Variation: Collard greens or swish chard can also be used.

*Victoria Moran is the author of many books that aid in *Living a Charmed Life*, the title of one of her books. Her latest is *Main Street Vegan*.

Dilip's Lime Jerk Seitan

Serves 4

Created by Dilip Barman, head of the Triangle Vegetarian Society in North Carolina, and host of the largest annual vegan Thanksgiving feast in the USA with over 800 attendees. For more information, see **www.trianglevegsociety. org** and **www.dilipdinner.blogspot.com.**

MARINADE

Seitan	**8** ounces, cubed
Lime	**1**, juiced
Garlic	**3** to 4 cloves, pressed
Fresh oregano	**10** leaves, torn into small pieces (or dried oregano, $1/8$ teaspoon)

Combine all marinade ingredients in a bowl and allow to set 2–3 hours or overnight in the refrigerator.

JERK SPICES

Chili powder, garlic powder	$1/4$ to $1/2$ teaspoon each
Salt, oregano, allspice, nutmeg	$1/8$ teaspoon each

Mix spices for jerk in a small bowl and set aside.

VEGETABLES

Olive oil	**1** to 2 teaspoons
Kale	**1** bunch, stems diced and leaves torn into pieces, divided
Onion	**1** medium, diced
Bell pepper, red or orange	**1**, diced

Add olive oil to large skillet and heat over medium-high heat. Drain marinade and sauté seitan in a single layer for 4–5 minutes, or until light brown on all sides. Add diced kale stems and cook about 1 minute. Add onion and sauté until caramelized. Add bell pepper and kale leaves and cook an additional 1–2 minutes. Mix in jerk seasonings, blending well.

SUPER POWERFUL SWEET POTATOES

Count the ways to eat a sweet potato—baked or roasted, mashed, candied, grilled, fried, boiled, steamed, made into chips—and super-packed with dense nutrition, a true super food!

JUST SOME OF THEIR GOODNESS
Beta-carotene; the darker the orange the greater the value
Vitamin A, huge amounts, good for eyesight and skin
Vitamin C, protects against infection
Fiber, lowers cholesterol and assists digestion
Surprisingly improves blood sugar regulation

PREPARATION
Do not store raw potatoes in the refrigerator.

Boiled: They can be cubed and added to soups (homemade or canned) where there is liquid ready to cook them.

They can be boiled whole and unpeeled (since many nutrients are just beneath the skin) and are easy to peel after cooking. Wash them; puncture each one to allow any steam to escape during cooking. Add to a saucepan, cover with water, add a pinch of salt, and boil gently until tender. Drain, peel, and eat as is or flavor with any of the following; favorite herbs or spices, such as cumin, cloves, curry powder, salt and pepper, oil, or vegan margarine. This is the stage they can also be mashed.

Mashed: Follow instructions for boiling above. Add some soy milk, or other milk alternative, and vegan margarine; mash with a potato masher or beat gently for a short time in a stand mixer for a fluffier version. They may be soft enough to just mash without adding a milk alternative, if desired.

Using as a sandwich spread is incredibly and surprisingly wonderful. Mix some nut butter (almond or cashew) with it for an even more nutrient and flavor punch.

Microwaved: Wash potatoes and using a fork or sharp knife, pierce at any place on the potato to allow steam to escape during cooking. Place them on a paper towel in the microwave. It is easier to cook 2 at a time on high for 8–10 minutes. For more potatoes, increase the time. Be especially careful when removing from the oven. Allow to cool and then peel for whatever dish you are preparing.

Grilled: Preheat grill, indoors or out, and lightly oil grill or grate. Peel potatoes and cut potatoes crosswise into ¹/₂-inch or 1-inch medallions. Coat them with oil or cooking spray and season with salt. Grill each side for about 10 minutes or until tender. Lightly coat with vegan margarine. Sprinkle with spices like garam masala (Indian mix), cumin, cinnamon, ginger, Old Bay Seasoning, Cajun spice, chili powder, or other favorite; or sweeten with brown sugar or maple syrup.

Fried: See Better For You Fries (page 89) and simply substitute sweet potatoes for the white potatoes.

Maple Butter Roasted Sweet Potatoes
Serves 10

Yoli Ouiya* is a young woman with super energy and immersed in green living. She offers a sweet potato recipe full of nutrition.

MAPLE BUTTER

Vegan margarine (Earth Balance, Smart Balance Light)	**1** cup, softened
Maple syrup, pure	¹/₂ cup

Beat margarine at high-speed until light and fluffy. Gradually beat in syrup until well blended.

ROASTED SWEET POTATOES

Sweet potatoes	3¹/₂ pounds, peeled, halved, and cut into ¹/₂-inch pieces
Olive oil	**2** tablespoons
Sea salt and pepper	to taste

Preheat oven to 375 degrees and position rack in bottom third of oven. In a large bowl, coat potatoes with olive oil and then spread on a baking sheet.

Roast for about 30 minutes, turning midway through. Drop spoonfuls of maple butter onto yams and continue roasting until glazed, about 25 minutes. Add salt and pepper.

Note: Potatoes can be roasted without the maple butter and stored until ready to use. Reheat in oven until just warmed through and add maple butter.

*See her site at **www.yolisgreenliving.com**, an eco-chic guide for all aspects of life.

Stovetop Candied Sweet Potatoes

Serves 4

Many people bake their candied potatoes but I enjoy getting them done quickly on the stovetop. They can be reheated, but because of the cornstarch used, the candied syrup becomes a bit jelled. There is never a holiday without this dish on the table.

Sweet potato*	1 large or 2 medium, peeled
Water	2 cups
Salt	1/4 teaspoon
Vegan margarine	2 tablespoons
Maple syrup, pure	1/4 cup
Cornstarch and water	1/4 cup each

Cut potato crosswise into 1-inch slices and then cut each slice into quarters. Place in a saucepan and add water and salt. Bring to boil for 8–10 minutes and then turn to medium heat until fork tender. Turn heat down and add margarine and syrup and stir around sides of the pan, lifting from bottom upward to keep the potato pieces as undisturbed as possible. Mix cornstarch and water in a cup to create a slurry. Add to pan and stir in same way until thickened. Do not allow to boil as it can break the cornstarch and it will not thicken, or could lose thickness.

*Canned yams can be used, adding the juice as well to the saucepan. Most canned sweet potatoes are labeled yams. Note that brown sugar can be used instead of maple syrup.

Roasted Sweet Potatoes and Chickpeas

Serves 4

Chef Chad Sarno has opened vegan restaurants in the USA and in foreign countries. As Senior Culinary Educator with Whole Foods Market, he helped create their Health Starts Here Program. He is also a celebrated raw vegan chef.

Sweet potatoes, cubed	**3** cups
Red onion	**1** small, diced
Olive oil	**3** tablespoons
Rosemary	**2** tablespoons
Chile flakes	**¼** teaspoon
Sea salt	**1** teaspoon
Chickpeas, cooked	**1½** cups or 2 (15-ounce) cans, drained and rinsed
Tomato, diced	**1** cup
Parsley, fresh, chopped	**¼** cup
Pepper	to taste

Preheat oven to 375 degrees. In a large bowl, toss sweet potato, onion, olive oil, rosemary, chile flakes, and salt; spread on baking sheet. Roast for 15 minutes and remove from oven. Add chickpeas and tomatoes, spreading out evenly on baking sheet. Continue to roast for another 15 minutes or until sweet potatoes are fork tender. Remove from oven, toss with parsley and pepper.

Sweet Potato Chips

A way to have chips and feel good about it!

Sweet potatoes	**2** medium, thinly sliced
Olive oil	**1** tablespoon
Sea salt	to taste

Preheat oven to 400 degrees. In a large bowl, drizzle potatoes with oil and spread in a single layer on baking sheets. Bake until edges are crispy and the centers are still soft, about 25 minutes, turning once during baking. Sprinkle with salt.

SIMPLY SQUASH

WINTER SQUASH

All hard-skinned winter squash, such as butternut, acorn, kabocha, delicata, spaghetti, hubbard, calabash, and others have many things in common:

Full of beta-carotene, iron, vitamins

0 cholesterol, 0 fat, 2 grams protein in 1 cup of cubed squash, 82 calories per cup

457% of daily requirement of vitamin A and 50% of vitamin C

Hard protective skin can be eaten if softened enough by cooking

Heavy for its size, usually orange or yellow inside

All require similar cooking methods

Often interchangeable in recipes

Varying sweetness which can also be related to age

COOKING

Baked or Roasted: Wash well. Most all squash can be cooked by cutting in half, scraping out the seeds, rubbing oil or vegan margarine over the flesh, and placing cut side up on a baking pan. Add an inch or so of water, baking at 375 degrees for about 30–60 minutes depending on the size of the squash, until fork tender. Alternative method: place squash cut side down on baking sheet and bake the same way, eliminating the water. Some cooks like to have a little water in this method as well and use no oil.

Many flavorings can be added before or after baking or roasting. Examples: salt, pepper, brown sugar, maple sugar, cinnamon, or ginger, garlic, dried fruit, herbs, and so on.

Steamed or Boiled: Wash well. Peel with a good potato peeler; remove seeds and cut into small chunks. Add 1-inch water and 1/2 teaspoon salt to a saucepan, cover, and bring to a boil. Add squash, cover, and cook 15–30 minutes, depending on size and age of squash. Use a steaming basket if you have one.

Sautéed: Wash well. Peel with a good potato peeler, remove seeds, and cut into slices or chunks. Sauté in a skillet with vegetable stock, vegan margarine, or a small amount of vegetable oil over medium-high heat until fork tender. Add salt and pepper.

Servings: Usually allow 1/2 pound per serving, or 1/2 an acorn squash in size.

SUMMER SQUASH

Summer squash, such as zucchini, crookneck, and pattypan, are more delicate.
Eat the tender skins of summer squash for most nutrients.
Provides dietary fiber at 2.5 grams per cup, but it also provides
special benefits for blood sugar regulation.

COOKING

Steaming: This is the best method for nutrient retention for summer squash.
Place a small amount of water in a skillet, add squash, cover, and cook until
water has evaporated, adding more water, if needed, until squash is tender.

Sauté: Sauté in a healthy way, by heating about $1/4$ cup of vegetable broth
or water in a stainless steel skillet over medium heat. Add sliced squash and
sauté for a minute or so on each side. Add more liquid, if needed.

Microwave: Cut in half lengthwise, remove seeds, place flesh down on a
plate, pierce skin with a fork to allow steam to escape, cover with a damp paper
towel, and cook on high for 5–15 minutes based on size and desired texture.

Roasted Butternut Squash

Serves 6

Bobbi Boock tosses this together when she gets home from the office and then
preps everything else while it is roasting. Dinner in about 30 minutes.

Butternut squash	**1** medium
Brussels sprouts	**1** pound
Cauliflower	$1/2$ head
Broccoli	**1** bunch
Onion	**1** large
Olive oil	
Sea salt, cayenne or black pepper	

Preheat oven to 350 degrees. Wash, trim, and cut vegetables into bite-size
pieces. Toss with olive oil, salt, and pepper. Place in a greased baking pan and
roast $1/2$ hour or until tender. I suggest keeping the squash as the staple and
switching out most any winter vegetable as the market changes.

Countless Acorn Squash Recipes

Serving: ¹/₄ wedge or less per serving as a side dish. Use ¹/₂ squash for a main course.

From classic to creative—acorn (and other squash) allows for countless recipes dreamed up on the spot.

Follow instructions for one of the cooking methods on (page 76) and then add any of the following:

A light sprinkle of salt and pepper and a teaspoon of vegan margarine.

Drizzle with maple syrup and/or brown sugar (vegan Sucanat).

Add chopped dried cranberries, raisins, prunes, or other fruit.

Bake with some garlic cloves in the cavities.

Crumble vegan bacon along with any of the choices listed.

Drizzle with coconut milk before serving.

Lightly pour on a bit of a favorite salad dressing.

Sprinkle with nutmeg or cinnamon.

Or, a drizzle of Grand Marnier or Amaretto.

Spaghetti Squash with Spaghetti Sauce

Serves 4

This is the most unique of all squash. It is really fun to eat.

Spaghetti squash	1, cut in half and seeds removed
Extra virgin olive oil	3 tablespoons
Vegan sausage, ground (Lightlife's Gimme Lean)	¹/₄ cup
Onion	1 small, chopped
Garlic	2 cloves, thinly sliced
Mushrooms, button, sliced	¹/₂ cup, optional
Spaghetti sauce	1 (24-ounce) jar

Preheat oven to 350 degrees. Place spaghetti squash cut side down in a baking dish and add 1 inch of water. Bake until the flesh of the squash is tender when pierced with a fork, about 45 minutes or longer depending on size.

Meanwhile, warm oil in a large skillet over medium heat. Stir in vegan sausage, onion, and garlic; cook about 5 minutes, occasionally stirring. Add mushrooms, if using, and cook for 3 more minutes. Stir in spaghetti sauce. Cover and simmer while the squash bakes.

When the squash is ready, drag a fork through the flesh from one end to the other, coaxing it into strands. Empty onto a plate. Top with desired amount of sauce and serve.

Mashed Kabocha Squash with Toasted Coconut

Serves 4

Brendon Brazier, Ironman competitor, is proof that athletes do extremely well on plant diets. His latest book, *Thrive Foods*, assists everyone in getting to great health.

Coconut, shredded	$1/4$ cup
Kabocha squash	**1** pound, cooked
Light coconut milk	**3** tablespoons
Salt and pepper	to taste

In a small skillet over medium-low heat, toast the coconut for 1–2 minutes, stirring constantly, until golden brown. Coconut burns easily, so remove from heat immediately after cooking. Mash the squash and coconut milk together with a fork or handheld mixer. Season with salt and pepper, if desired, and top with toasted coconut.

AND DON'T FORGET PUMPKINS!

They are not just jack-o-lanterns or pumpkin pie. Buy the whole pumpkin, or canned, and use as any other squash preparation.

1 cup mashed pumpkin yields: 49 calories, 0 cholesterol, low fat and sodium, vitamin A, E, and C, and fiber.

GRAINS! GRAINS! GRAINS!

Grains are so power-packed that they are being named three times. What do they bring us?

PROTEIN and FIBER are the biggies—usually from 6–14 grams of protein and 5–9 grams of fiber per cup, depending on the grain. Fiber is the complex carbohydrate that "clean sweeps" the digestive tract. (Animal products have no fiber.) Magnesium is the other nutrient common in all grains, and there are a host of others packed into the various members of the grain family.

COOKING GRAINS

Place water or vegetable broth in a saucepan

Bring to boil (with about $1/2$ teaspoon salt, if desired[*])

Add grain

Cover

Lower heat

Cook specified time for that particular grain

Allow to rest a few minutes after cooking, covered

Fluff with a fork

[*]You can add salt to grains during cooking. (Hold the salt for beans—salt seems to hinder cooking to full tenderness.)

GRAIN	DRY MEASURE	WATER	COOKING TIME	YIELD
WHITE RICE	1 cup dry	2 cups water	15–20 minutes	3 cups
BROWN RICE	1 cup dry	$2^1/2$ cups water	45–55 minutes	3 cups
QUINOA	1 cup dry	2 cups water	15–20 minutes	$2^3/4$ cups
PEARL BARLEY	1 cup dry	3 cups water	50–60 minutes	$3^1/2$ cups
BULGUR WHEAT	1 cup dry	2 cups water	15 minutes[*]	$2^1/2$ cups

[*]Or, merely soak bulgur wheat in warm water for an hour to soften for salads.

These are only a few of the popular grains, also use spelt, millet, farro, kamut, oats, rye, various wheats (couscous, whole berries, cracked, bulgur), etc.

See **www.vegparadise.com/charts** for both grains and beans. There are helpful tips: how much water is needed to cook one cup of grains; how long to cook; and the yield after cooking.

Times can vary based on the age of the grain and the pan being used. Some pans are better heat conductors than others. Test at the end of cooking to see if tender enough. Add a small amount of water, if needed.

It is generally wise to allow the covered grain to cook without stirring as that activity can cause an undesired texture. When checking for liquid absorption near the end of cooking, gently push grains apart once with a spoon.

If some grains remain stuck to the bottom of the pan after serving, remove from heat, add a small amount of water, cover tightly, and allow to sit for a few minutes. The steam will release the remaining grains. This also allows for easy pot cleaning! (Use this same method if it happens when overcooking oatmeal or heating a soup too long.)

TIME-SAVING OPTIONS

Soak grains in the eventual cooking liquid for a few hours. Once cooking, watch for doneness along the way since the cooking time will be shortened.

Cook additional servings at the same time as grains can last nearly a week in the refrigerator. Reheat with additional water, or serve cold.

After the initial recipe, leftovers can be sprinkled on salads, added to soups, or simply served with salad dressing, nuts, and/or vegetables for a new meal.

Quinoa with Cashews

Serves 4–6

The intriguing John Joseph* of the Cro-Mags, offered this basic go-to quinoa recipe that can be created anew every time.

Quinoa is among the oldest grains in history. It is considered a perfect protein, meaning it has all 9 essential amino acids. It is also high in magnesium that relaxes blood vessels, making it good for heart disease, diabetes, and migraine headaches. It is also gluten-free.

Quinoa (traditional or red or mixed)	**1** cup
Water	**2** cups
Cashews, broken in pieces	**¹/₂** cup
Salt	**¹/₂** teaspoon
Turmeric	a pinch

Place quinoa in a mesh sieve and run cold water over the grains to rinse well. Bring water, cashews, salt, and turmeric to a boil. Add quinoa then stir and lower heat. Cover and simmer over low heat for 10–15 minutes until water evaporates. Serve hot or cold.

Variations: You can add any of the following to make this dish something new each time you make it; various vegetables, dried fruit, fresh fruit, and seeds like pumpkin or sunflower, or salad dressings, of choice.

*John Joseph is a former boxer and singer with the historic punk rock group, Cro-Mags. He is training for Ironman Triathlons and rocking mosh pits worldwide after the age of 50!

Quinoa Tabbouleh
Serves 4

Christine Waltermyer owns the Natural Kitchen Cooking School in New Jersey where she provides in-depth training in natural foods cooking. This recipe is a glorious example of how to use a grain and add refreshing ingredients that support great health—not to mention it's easy.

Vegetable broth	2 cups
Orange juice	2 cups
Quinoa	2 cups, rinsed
Parsley	1 bunch, stemmed
Fresh mint	1/4 cup
Cucumber	1 small, seeded, cut into 1- to 2-inch pieces
Sun-dried tomatoes	1/4 cup, soaked to soften
Olive oil	1/4 cup
Fresh lemon juice	1/2 cup
Sea salt and pepper	to taste

Pour vegetable broth and orange juice into a medium-size saucepan and bring to boil over medium-high heat. Add quinoa, cover, and reduce to low heat. Simmer for 20 minutes or until quinoa is fluffy and soft.

Place parsley, mint, cucumber, and tomatoes in a food processor or blender. Pulse until everything is finely chopped. Transfer cooked quinoa to a large mixing bowl. Cool slightly before adding parsley mixture. Add olive oil, lemon juice, salt, and pepper. Serve chilled.

Fabulous Barley Salad

Serves 12

Cathy DeVries is very social in her community and often attends potluck events. This is a friend-sharing-with-a-friend recipe and she shared it with me.

10-minute barley*	1 box
Olive oil	3 tablespoons
Onions	3 medium, vertically sliced
Garlic	3 cloves, peeled and minced

Curry powder	**1** tablespoon
Parsley, chopped	**2** tablespoons
Currants or raisins or craisins	**1** cup
Almonds, slivered	**1** cup
Salt and pepper	**1** teaspoon each

Cook barley per box instructions. Set aside. Heat oil in non-stick pan; add onions and cook about 10 minutes. Stir in garlic, cooking for another 5 minutes. Add some water, if needed, to complete cooking and to cut down on the oil. Add remaining ingredients. Reduce heat for about for 3 minutes. Add barley and toss. Serve warm or cold.

*For regular pearled barley, use 1 cup and 3 cups water, 50–60 minutes cooking time, yields 3 1/2 cups.

Heather Mills' Sesame Soba Noodles with Peanut Dressing

Serves 4

This is a perfect recipe for everyone, but certainly is a great way to get children to have a high protein plant dish using peanuts and buckwheat noodles (soba). This is from her book, *Love Bites*.

DRESSING

Peanuts, raw	1 cup
Nondairy milk (rice, soy, or almond)	5 tablespoons
Soy sauce	5 tablespoons
Tahini	5 tablespoons
Sesame oil	1/4 cup
Sake or white wine, rice wine, or apple cider vinegar	2 tablespoons
Maple syrup	5 tablespoons
Gingerroot, grated	1 tablespoon
Garlic	4 cloves, smashed

NOODLES

Soba noodles, regular spaghetti, or linguine	1 package
Sesame oil	3 teaspoons (only if making crispy noodles version)

Mix ingredients for dressing in a blender; if too thick, gradually add a little hot water. Set aside.

Cook noodles in boiling water for 7 minutes; drain in a colander and rinse with cold water. (For crispy noodles, cook noodles in hot sesame oil in a wok or large skillet for 5 minutes. However, if not using to crisp the noodles, drizzle 1/4 teaspoon of sesame oil over the newly rinsed noodles to make it easier to blend the peanut sauce with the noodles.)

Spread about a half cup of dressing in the bottom of a bowl; add noodles. With a spatula, gently lift some dressing up from the bottom and gently coax into the noodles. Add more dressing, as desired.

South African Yellow Rice

Serves 6

A dish with brown basmati rice, raisins, and a cinnamon stick! Cookbook author and chef, Bryanna Clark Grogan,* plows new ground for vegan cuisine with her latest *World Vegan Cuisine*. I was interested in a new way to use rice and found it with her help by "journeying" to South Africa. There, it is called Geel Rys.

Brown basmati rice, uncooked	2 cups
Vegetable broth	3 cups
Vegan margarine or olive oil	2 tablespoons
Onion	2 medium, minced
Garlic	2 cloves, minced
Turmeric	1 teaspoon
Raisins	1/2 to 3/4 cup
Sugar	2 tablespoons
Cinnamon stick	1

Eight hours before cooking the rice, combine the rice with the vegetable broth in a medium pot or bowl and cover.

Preheat oven to 375 degrees.

In a large skillet, heat the margarine and sauté the onions until quite soft, about 10 minutes, adding drops of water as necessary to keep from sticking or browning. Add to a 2- to 3-quart casserole baking dish and stir in the soaked rice and broth; add the remaining ingredients. Cover and bake for 45 minutes. Serve hot.

A vegan meatloaf is usually served with this dish in South Africa. See The Other Proteins section and choose Maple-Ginger Baked Tofu Cutlets (page 111) or Rotisserie-Style Tempeh (page 107).

* Bryanna Clark Grogan's site, **www.bryannaclarkgrogan.com,** is filled with links, recipes, and articles that will aid anyone's journey for good information.

SIDES TO RELY ON

Sides often make up the main dish for vegans. Here are some basic recipes that can be used in combinations to make a meal or to round out a meal.

Fluffy Mashed Potatoes

Serves 4–6

This is how my parents made their fluffy mashed potatoes at our diner. Perfectly smooth and fluffy mashed potatoes are easy but take some explaining to avoid pitfalls.

Red potatoes	**6** medium
Salt	**1/2** teaspoon in cooking water
Soy milk	**1/2** cup, approximately
Vegan margarine (Earth Balance or Smart Balance Light)	**2** to **3** tablespoons

Peel the potatoes and cover with water in a saucepan. Add salt. Boil until fork tender, about 20 minutes. Lift one by one with a slotted spoon into the bowl of a stand mixer. If using a hand mixer, you can drain and then return to the hot pot for mashing.

Start the beaters on low just to gently break up the potatoes to a rough mash. (Never put the beaters on high to avoid gummy potatoes.) Add some of the soy milk. Potatoes hold water, so they might already be moist.

Continue to beat on low and add the margarine. Add more soy milk, if needed. Keep in mind that as the potatoes cool they become slightly thicker. Taste to see if salt is needed. Whip at medium speed to incorporate air for only a few seconds and done!

Tal's Cashew-Cream Mashed Potatoes

From *The Conscious Cook* by Tal Ronnen

Serves 4

If there were a James Beard Award for a vegan chef, it would go to Tal Ronnen, and I would be there to applaud the event! He elevates vegan food to a fine cuisine.

Potatoes, white	**5** medium, peeled and diced
Cashew Cream (see below)	**1/3** cup or more if desired (allow time to soak cashews overnight *)
Vegan margarine	**2** tablespoons
Chives, fresh, minced	**2** tablespoons
Sea salt and freshly ground pepper	to taste

Place potatoes in a large pot, cover with water, and bring to a boil. Cook, uncovered, for 10–15 minutes, until tender; drain. Place the potatoes in a mixer and beat, using whisk attachment. Add Cashew Cream, margarine, and chives. Whip at medium-high speed, seasoning with salt and pepper, just until smooth and fluffy.

CASHEW CREAM

Makes 3 1/2 cups

Used for mashed potatoes in this recipe, it has many other uses, such as adding to soup for a wonderful creamy base. See Tal's book for many more dishes and uses.

Cashews, whole, raw	**2** cups, rinsed very well under cold water

Place cashews into a bowl with enough cold water to cover them. Cover bowl and refrigerate overnight. Drain and rinse with cold water. Place in a blender with enough cold water to cover them by 1 inch. Blend on high for several minutes until very smooth. If not using a high powered blender, it might be necessary to strain cashew cream through a fine mesh sieve. To make a thick cashew cream, reduce amount of water in blender so it just covers the cashews.

*A second option is to boil them, remove from heat, and soak for an hour, but this method does leach out some sweetness of the nuts.

Better-For-You Fries

Serves 6–8

Everyone's guilty pleasure is French fries. These will become another one with less guilt!

Potatoes (red or Yukon gold) .... **4** large
Olive oil or other vegetable oil .... **1** tablespoon
Seasonings mix .... $^1/_4$ to $^1/_2$ teaspoon of any or
    all of the following: chili powder, dried basil, dried oregano, garlic or
    onion powder, garlic salt, cayenne pepper, hot pepper sauce, and paprika.
    Amount depends on preference for flavor and spice. Or, if in a rush, just
    sprinkle with Old Bay Seasoning.

Preheat oven to 450 degrees. Wash potatoes and cut lengthwise into wedges and or spears. Dry potatoes.

In a large bowl, mix oil and seasonings; add potatoes and toss well. Spread potatoes in a single layer on a lightly oiled baking sheet. Bake 20–30 minutes until fork tender, turning halfway through. Salt, if needed.

Picnic Potato Salad

Serves 4–6

Potato salads are influenced by family tradition, heritage, and personal tastes. This one is a fast basic recipe that can be expanded in more adventurous directions!

Potatoes (new potatoes or Yukon gold)	4 medium
Salt	to taste
Garlic	1 clove, smashed, optional
Onion (white or red), small dice	1/2 cup
Celery	2 stalks, small dice

DRESSING

Soy milk (plain or vanilla)	1/4 cup
Vegan mayonnaise	3/4 cup (silken tofu of equal amount can be a substitute)
Mustard, prepared	1/2 teaspoon
Pepper (black, white, or cayenne)	to taste
Salt	1/4 teaspoon, optional

Peel the potatoes or not, your choice. In large saucepan, cover whole potatoes with water and add salt and garlic, if using. Boil until just fork tender, about 20 minutes. Transfer potatoes to a bowl to cool.

In the meantime, make the dressing. In a small bowl, add soy milk very gradually into the mayonnaise; add mustard, pepper, and salt.

When cool, cut potatoes into bite-size cubes. Place in a large bowl and add onion and celery. Carefully fold in dressing with a spatula to combine. Flavors meld better if allowed to set in the refrigerator for a few hours or overnight.

Variations: Stir 2–3 tablespoons horseradish into the dressing, or add crumbled vegan bacon, ground caraway seeds, chopped parsley, dill pickle juice, red bell pepper, curry powder, or even chopped grapes.

Warm Potato Salad with Spinach and Red Peppers

Serves 8

It is a delight when you visit a place that might not be so vegan-friendly and have an exciting dish. This recipe is based on Chef John Wassil's salad, from Bistro 72, Chambersburg, PA.

Potatoes (red or russet)	**4** medium, bite-size pieces
Bell pepper, red	**1** medium, seeded and diced
Vegetable oil	**1** teaspoon
Vegetable broth or water	**1** tablespoon or more
Garlic, finely chopped	**1** tablespoon (1 to 2 cloves)
Onion, finely chopped	**1** tablespoon
Spinach leaves	**2** large handfuls
Salt and pepper	to taste

Boil potatoes in salted water until tender, about 10 minutes; drain.

In large skillet, sauté bell pepper in oil and vegetable broth over medium heat, about 10 minutes. When almost done, add garlic and onion and cook gently, being careful not to burn mixture, adding more broth, if needed. Reduce heat to low, add spinach and cover; allow spinach to wilt. Add potatoes and toss; adjust for salt and pepper.

Corn on the Cob

Makes as much as you need!

Corn on the cob is best in season. Many people fill a pot with salted water and completely immerse the cobs and then overcook and pour important nutrients down the drain. To hold in flavor and food values, consider grilling or steaming as first options.

Corn on the cob, fresh
Vegan margarine or vegetable oil
Salt

To grill on stovetop, heat a grill and coat with the smallest amount of margarine or vegetable oil, place corn on the grill, and use tongs to turn the cobs as they brown. The sweetness of the corn will help the caramelization. On an outside grill, you can leave in husks (remove most outer dry ones) and char on all sides for about 20 minutes.

To steam, add about a 1/2-inch water to a skillet or flat pan and add a pinch of salt. Add corn and heat to steaming, using a tight lid for about 3 minutes. Done. It can taste so good this way that to add anything, even a bit of margarine, might be too disruptive to the sweetness.

To microwave, leave in husks, cook for 1 minute, turn, and heat for 1 more minute. Rest for about 3 minutes.

To freeze, buy in season and use the steaming method. Cut kernels off cob and put into freezer-safe containers with top space for freezing expansion. Enjoy all winter!

Eat raw. Yes! If you are lucky to be at a farmers market where the corn was just picked, treat yourself to a good healthy bite and be in a state of pleasure and surprise!

Steamed Whole Carrots

Makes however much you need!

This is the basic cooking method for most vegetables, even leafy greens, but it is especially tasty with carrots.

Carrots, long with stems	2 to 3 carrots per person
Salt	$^1/_8$ teaspoon
Vegan margarine, smallest amount to lightly coat, optional	

Trim leaves from stems, leaving about 3 inches of stem. Peel skin if rough or for a smooth look. In a skillet or flat pan with a tight lid, add the carrots with $^1/_2$- to 1-inch water and salt. Cover and steam over medium heat until fork tender, about 10 minutes. Serve on a platter and brush margarine on the carrots to add flavor as well as a moist appearance.

This is the basic cooking and seasoning method. From this point, allow personal tastes to dictate adding other flavors, such as chopped parsley, rosemary, or garlic. Some prefer sweet additions, but carrots are sweet to begin with and it can be distracting to their stand-alone wonderfulness.

Brussels Sprouts with Walnuts and Croutons

Serves 4

This is a lovely way to enjoy Brussels sprouts.

Brussels sprouts	1 pound, cut in half
Vegetable oil	1 tablespoon
Vegetable stock or water	$^1/_4$ cup
Vinegar	a drizzle
Walnuts, coarsely chopped	$^1/_4$ cup
Garlic	1 clove, minced
Bread	2 slices, cubed (crusts removed)

Once Brussels sprouts are cut, allow them to set for about 10 minutes to activate special enzymes which have additional health benefits in them. Cutting in quarters is even better. Add oil and stock to a skillet and place Brussels sprouts cut-side down. Cover and cook over medium heat, until browned and slightly softened, trying not to stir for about 20–30 minutes. Do not allow to burn. Add more oil or stock, if needed. Remove the sprouts to a bowl and drizzle with the vinegar. Add walnuts, garlic, and bread cubes to the skillet and brown. Add more oil, if needed. Toss into sprouts and serve.

Braised Celery

Serves 4

We certainly take celery for granted. We eat it raw as a snack, juiced for vegetable drinks, and filled with something as an appetizer. Braising is a great way to cook it. Celery is good for reducing blood pressure, is a source of vitamin K and C as well as potassium, folate, and of course, fiber.

Celery	**8** stalks
Water	$^1/_2$ cup
Sea salt	$^1/_4$ teaspoon
Pepper	$^1/_4$ teaspoon
Vegetable broth	$^1/_2$ cup

With a peeler, shave any course parts on the stalks. Cut each stalk into diagonal pieces, about an inch, and reserve the leaves. Add celery, water, salt, and pepper to a skillet and cook over medium heat, about 2 minutes. Add broth, if needed. Cover and reduce heat to low and cook until celery is just tender. Uncover and cook until the liquid has been reduced to a glaze. Top with reserved leaves.

Mushroom and Herb Sauté

Serves 4

Mushrooms come in many varieties. Most all are prepared similarly. Do not stir much if sautéing, allow juices to come out. All are low-calorie alone and can be eaten raw or cooked. If you need some B vitamins and good minerals, eat mushrooms. Many use mushrooms as a meat substitute in meals for the texture.

Extra virgin olive oil	**2** tablespoons

Mushrooms, button	about 15 ounces, stems removed, sliced or chopped
Salt and pepper	¼ teaspoon each
Garlic	1 clove, sliced
Vegan margarine	1 tablespoon
Thyme leaves, fresh	1 teaspoon or ¼ teaspoon dried
Wine, white dry, or water	¼ cup
Parsley, fresh, chopped	1 tablespoon

In a large skillet, add oil over medium-high heat. Sauté mushrooms without stirring, until caramelized, about 5 minutes. Add salt and pepper and combine with mushrooms, cook until browned. Add garlic, margarine, and thyme and cook until golden. Slowly add wine and allow to evaporate. Add parsley and serve.

Sautéed Mixed Greens

Serves 2 or 4 small servings

This is such a basic recipe, but it is also one that can be depended upon often. Switch out the greens for whatever might be at the market or in your adventurous spirit.

Olive oil	2 tablespoons
Garlic	3 cloves, thinly sliced
Collard greens	½ bunch, rinsed, stemmed, and chopped
Kale	½ bunch, rinsed, stemmed, and chopped

Heat oil in a large skillet over medium-high heat. Add garlic and sauté until tender, about 2 minutes. Add the greens and sauté another 3 minutes until wilted. Serve at once.

Variations: Use chard and mustard greens. For fat-free, add about a ½-inch water to the skillet, instead of oil, in order to steam rather than sauté, and add the garlic at the same time.

Dixie Diner's Creamy Coleslaw

Serves 6

Although this seems to be a casual dish, I find that even at elegant dinners the coolness of coleslaw goes so well with potatoes, breaded items, and spicy dishes. Do not be concerned if taking on a picnic as there is no dairy to spoil.

Vegan mayonnaise or a combination with vegan sour cream	¼ cup
Vinegar (apple cider or favorite light)	¼ cup
Sugar, evaporated cane juice	1 to 2 tablespoons
Mustard, prepared	⅛ teaspoon, optional
Cabbage, shredded	4 cups
Carrot	1 medium, grated

Combine first 4 ingredients in a large bowl. Add cabbage and carrots and mix well. Eat immediately, but storing overnight seems to blend the flavors well.

Thanks to my sister, Aileen Sharar, for retrieving from our diner recipe archives.

Broccoli with "Cheese" Sauce

Serves 4–6

I was hoping to have a good broccoli dish with a cheesy sauce that was on our menus before being vegan. From her *Big Vegan* cookbook, Robin Asbell, offered this one. We already know the powers of broccoli as an immune booster and that it is power packed with vitamin C, but keep in mind that it is a member of the brassica family with super relatives; kale, cabbage, Brussels sprouts, and bok choy.

Broccoli, fresh	1 pound
Rice milk, plain, or other nondairy milk on hand	1 cup
Nutritional yeast	¼ cup
Dijon mustard	1½ teaspoons

Garlic	1 clove, minced
Salt	$1/2$ teaspoon
Paprika	pinch
Vegan margarine	2 tablespoons
Flour, unbleached	2 tablespoons

Wash and cut broccoli into long spears including stems. Prepare a steamer or use a skillet with lid and add about $1/2$ cup water with a pinch of salt. Do not steam until the sauce is made.

Whisk rice milk, nutritional yeast, mustard, garlic, salt, and paprika together in a small bowl to have ready for the sauce.

In a small saucepan, melt margarine over low heat. Whisk in flour, forming a roux, until bubbly. Take off heat and very gradually whisk in a little of the milk mixture at a time, being sure it is smooth each time. Return to medium heat and constantly whisk as sauce slowly comes to a boil and thickens. Remove from heat and cover with a lid to stay warm while steaming the broccoli. Turn heat to medium high to steam broccoli until fork tender, for about 3–5 minutes, depending on size of broccoli pieces. Serve broccoli topped with sauce.

PROTEIN-RICH BEANS AND LENTILS

LEGUMES

They are steak in a little pod. Here are some interesting facts:
Protein, but with no dangerous saturated fat and cholesterol!
The nutrients to aid in prevention of heart disease, cancer, and
    obesity.
Tons of FIBER!
Rich in complex carbohydrates, vitamins, and minerals.
There are over 1,000 legumes, but we have settled on the most
    popular varieties of beans, peas, and lentils, which includes soy
    and garbanzo beans (chickpeas).
Easily absorbs the flavors of herbs and spices.
Good for the environment as they fix the atmospheric nitrogen in
    the soil.
Found in 5,000-year-old settlements in the Middle East and other
    countries, certainly a well-proven source of good nutrients.
    And, so economical in costs!

SOY BEANS

Just two servings or more a day can help strengthen or rebuild bones, help
retain calcium, result in less secretion in the urine that dairy products cause,
and offer all the other good aspects of ingesting legumes. Consider soy milk,
edamame, miso broth, tofu, or tempeh.

PREPPING

See Basic Prep For Your Vegetables, Greens, Grains, Nuts, and Beans (pages
21–24) for cooking instructions. But basically . . .
A pound of beans will serve 6–8 people, if 1 serving is 3/4 to 1 cup.
A cup of dry beans yields approximately 3 cups cooked.

Lentil Patties

Serves 4

Lentils are not only nutritious, they are a versatile food to put into a main course.

Water	2 cups
Red lentils	1 1/4 cups, washed and drained
Onion	1 medium, finely chopped
Olive oil	1 tablespoon or more
Salt and pepper	to taste
Whole-wheat flour	enough for coating

Preheat oven to 400 degrees. Bring water to a boil in a large saucepan and add lentils. Cover and simmer over low heat, about 15 minutes, stirring occasionally. Add water, if needed. Test by lifting out a few lentils and smash to see if they are soft in the center. Cook longer if needed.

Sauté onion in oil for about 10 minutes; add lentils, salt, and pepper. When cool enough to handle, form into patties of desired size, coating each with flour; place on greased baking sheet. Bake for about 30 minutes, turning over once midway.

Variation: Alternatively, add vegetable oil to skillet and fry patties until crisp; drain on paper towels.

4-Fold Mexican Sweet Potato and Black Bean Salad

Serves 16

Cathi DiCocoa has a restaurant and bakery in Bethel, ME, and she is the most enthusiastic vegan chef one can imagine. She offers one of her most popular recipes at Café DiCocoa, served four different ways.

SALAD

Sweet potatoes	8 medium, peeled and diced into chunks

Canola oil	3 to 4 tablespoons
Ground coriander, cumin, chili powder, and salt	1 teaspoon each
Corn	4 cups
Black beans	4 cups, cooked
Scallions	6 to 8, thinly sliced
Fresh cilantro, chopped	1 cup

DRESSING

Chipotle chiles (from canned chipotle in adobe sauce)	2
Garlic	2 cloves, minced
Thai sweet chili sauce	$^1/_4$ cup
Limes	6 medium, juiced (about $^3/_4$ cup)
Canola oil	1 cup

Preheat oven to 375 degrees. In a large bowl, toss sweet potato with canola oil to lightly coat. Sprinkle in spices and toss again. Spread a single layer on a baking sheet with sides and roast until golden around the edges and just tender, about 15–20 minutes.

Microwave corn in a small amount of water, for 3–5 minutes; drain. Place corn and beans in large mixing bowl and add baked and slightly cooled sweet potatoes. Add scallions and cilantro.

To make dressing: Place chipotle chiles, garlic, and sweet chili sauce in a blender and blend until smooth. Add lime juice and blend again. Slowly add canola oil until emulsified. Add just enough to the salad to moisten.

Serve on fresh greens; roll in a soft tortilla with some greens; layer on a soft tortilla with grated vegan cheese, fold, and grill until brown, like a quesadilla; or add to chili with tomatoes and onions. To make a completely different dish, Cathi says, "substitute canned diced tomatoes for the sweet potatoes and you have a wickedly good salsa!"

Barbecued Beans with Candle 79's BBQ Sauce

Serves 4–6

Joy Pierson, Bart Potenza, and Benay Vynerib, along with Chefs Angel Ramos and Jorge Pineda, create magic at the top-rated Candle 79 in New York City. How lucky for us to get their barbecue sauce recipe.

Navy or northern beans	**2** (15-ounce) cans, drained and rinsed
Candle 79 BBQ Sauce (see below)	**1**^{1}/$_2$ to 2 cups
Vegan bacon (Lightlife)	**2** strips, cooked

Add beans to a saucepan with enough BBQ Sauce to just cover. Cook over medium heat until sauce slightly thickens, about 10 minutes. Add crumbled bacon. Refrigerate any remaining sauce.

CANDLE 79'S BBQ SAUCE

Yields 5 cups

Tomato paste	**1** cup
Ketchup	**1** cup
Tamari	^{1}/$_2$ cup
Molasses	^{1}/$_3$ cup
Brown rice vinegar	^{1}/$_4$ cup
Apple cider vinegar	^{1}/$_4$ cup
Water	^{3}/$_4$ cup
Maple syrup	^{1}/$_2$ cup
Tamarind paste	^{1}/$_4$ cup or 3 dates
Coriander powder or cumin	^{1}/$_2$ teaspoon
Chipotle powder	^{3}/$_4$ teaspoon

Place all ingredients into a blender and blend until smooth. Transfer to a sauté pan and cook 10 minutes on medium heat, stirring occasionally.

Vegetable Napoleon with White Bean Ragu and Sautéed Broccoli

Serves 4

Odyssey Cruise chef, Don Neff, graciously sent a lengthy recipe for this, and another great chef friend, Brian Kaywork, created a simpler version.

LAYERS

Tomato sauce, (Muirs organic)	**2** cups
White Bean Ragout	**3** cups (see below)
Broccoli, sautéed	**1** pound (see facing)
Olive tapenade (Meditalia vegan black olive)	**1/2** cup, optional
Corn tortillas	**12** (3 1/2-inch) rounds, toasted

WHITE BEAN RAGOUT

Olive oil	**3** tablespoons
Garlic	**2** cloves, minced
Rosemary, fresh, minced	**1** tablespoon
White beans	**2** (15-ounce) cans, drained
Water or vegetable stock	**1** cup

| Salt | 2 teaspoons |
| Pepper | 1 teaspoon |

Heat the oil and garlic in a medium pot until just lightly browned, about a minute. Add rosemary and stir 15 seconds. Add beans, water, salt, and pepper and simmer 10 minutes. Smash some of the beans to help thicken the remaining beans. Diced celery and carrots can be added.

SAUTÉED BROCCOLI

Olive oil	3 tablespoons
Garlic	2 cloves, sliced
Broccoli	1 pound, washed and chopped into 1-inch pieces
Red chili flakes	pinch, optional
Water	1 cup
Salt and pepper	to taste

Heat oil and garlic in a large skillet until lightly browned, about a minute. Add broccoli and chili flakes; stir. Add water and cook until evaporated or until barely fork tender. Add salt and pepper.

TOASTED TORTILLAS

Corn tortillas
Olive oil

Preheat oven to 400 degrees and brush both sides of tortillas with oil. Place on a baking sheet and toast for about 4 minute or until golden brown.

To plate: Place a bit of the tomato sauce on the plate, add a tortilla and top with ragu; top with another tortilla and top with some broccoli and a spoon of tomato sauce; top with the third tortilla and top with a spoon of the ragu and olive tapenade.

To make a bit more fancy, follow Chef Neff's idea of drizzling a balsamic glaze at the end. Combine 5 tablespoons balsamic vinegar, 1 tablespoon sugar, and $1/4$ teaspoon cayenne pepper in a saucepan and boil until it is reduced by half. Cool and drizzle over dish to finish. This can be used on many other dishes.

THE OTHER PROTEINS: TOFU, TEMPEH, AND SEITAN

PRONUNCIATIONS AND DEFINITIONS

TOFU (TOE'-foo)

This Asian process of coagulating soy milk and pressing into soft blocks is high in protein and calcium, low in fat and calories, and has no cholesterol.

Comparisons

Tofu, $^1/_2$ cup: 10 grams protein, 94 calories, 0 cholesterol, 5 grams fat, 227 milligrams calcium (based on processing)

Egg, $^1/_2$ cup chopped: 8 grams protein, 106 calories, 288 cholesterol, 7 grams fat, 32 milligrams calcium

Cheese, cheddar, $^1/_2$ cup diced: 16 grams protein, 266 calories, 70 milligrams cholesterol, 22 grams fat, 476 milligrams calcium

Ground beef, 75% raw lean, 3 ounces: 14 grams protein, 246 calories, 63 milligrams cholesterol, 21 grams fat, 18 milligrams calcium

Fish, cod, raw, 1 fillet: 20 grams protein, 95 calories, 43 milligrams cholesterol, .7 grams fat, 8 milligrams calcium

Source: **www.nutritiondata.self.com**

Two Primary Types

Silken: Japanese style and softer in texture (Mori-Nu brand is popular).

Comes in soft, firm, and extra firm and usually can be used interchangeably.

Sold in aseptic boxes on a shelf, not refrigerated.

Used for sauces, salad dressings, custards, and mayonnaise textures.

Regular: Chinese style and sturdier in texture (Nasoya is one brand).

Comes in soft, firm, and extra firm. Check recipes for best one.

Sold in sealed containers with water and found in the refrigerator.

Usually firm and extra firm are used for stir-frying, "cutlet" slices, and scrambles.

For a meatier chewy texture, freeze in unopened package, thaw, and squeeze out liquid, creating pores that will absorb the flavors of your recipe.

TEMPEH (TEM'-pay)

The fermenting process that binds soybeans into a flat bar, usually about 7 x $2^1/_2$ x $^3/_4$ inches (Lightlife is a popular brand) gives tempeh a meaty texture with a vague nutty or mushroom flavor. The process retains the whole bean, making it high in protein, fiber, and vitamins. Black or grey spores that can form are quite alright.

Some varieties come mixed with grains, vegetables, and seeds. All can be used interchangeably in recipes. It is more digestible than unprocessed soybeans.

See how to make your own through *New Farm Vegetarian Cookbook*, 2nd edition, by Louise Hagler and Dorothy R. Bates. It's not hard, it just takes care and time.

Comparisons

Tempeh, 3 ounces: 15 grams protein, 162 calories, 0 cholesterol, 9 grams fat, 93 milligrams calcium

Ground beef, 75% raw lean, 3 ounces: 14 grams protein, 246 calories, 63 milligrams cholesterol, 21 grams fat, 18 milligrams calcium

SEITAN (say-tan)

Wheat gluten, sometimes referred to as "wheat meat" (Westsoy and White Wave Foods are popular brands) has the protein of a steak without the fat and cholesterol.

Its soft chewy meat texture comes from over-working wheat dough and it can be purchased flavored or unflavored in shrink-wrapped packages in boxes. Seitan is sold in uneven strips, cutlets, or in roughly pulled apart pieces.

See how to make your own through Bryanna Clark Grogan's *World Vegan Feast,* pp. 5, 133.

Comparisons

Seitan, 3 ounces: 20 grams protein, 130 calories, 0 cholesterol, 1.5 grams fat (varies a bit by manufacturer)

Ground beef, 75% raw lean, 3 ounces: 14 grams protein, 246 calories, 63 milligrams cholesterol, 21 grams fat

Crispy Tofu and Rotisserie-Style Tempeh

Toni Fiori is host of Delicious TV's *Totally Vegetarian on Public Television* and is known for her doable vegan recipes that anyone can feel comfortable trying.

CRISPY TOFU

Serves 4

Tofu, extra firm	**1** package
Ground* rice (basmati, sushi, or jasmine)	**3** to **4** tablespoons
Coarse sea salt	**1** tablespoon
Pepper	**1/2** to **1** teaspoon
Cayenne or red pepper	**1/2** to **1** teaspoon
Coconut oil or neutral oil such as canola or safflower	

Drain and press tofu by wrapping in a towel then placing it on a plate topped with another plate and something slightly heavy like canned goods. Leave for 15 minutes to draw out moisture. Cut tofu into 4 (1-inch) slices; cut again corner to corner to form triangles.

In a shallow dish, mix rice, salt, and peppers. Coat tofu on all sides with the rice mixture. In a heavy skillet, pour in oil to about $^1/_2$ inch deep; heat a few minutes and test to be sure oil sizzles by slightly dipping in a corner of tofu. Fry tofu pieces until golden brown and crispy on all sides. Drain on paper towels. Serve hot or cold with your favorite condiments.

*Grind the rice in a food processor or blender until it is the texture of cornmeal.

ROTISSERIE-STYLE TEMPEH

Serves 4

Vegetable oil	**2** tablespoons
Rotisserie Spice Rub	**2** tablespoons (page 108)
Tempeh, any type	**8** ounces

Preheat oven to 400 degrees. In a medium bowl, combine the oil and Rotisserie Spice Rub. Cut the tempeh in half lengthwise. Cut the halves crosswise into desired pieces or cubes. Add the tempeh to the bowl and coat well. Place in a single layer into a baking dish and pour any remaining spice oil over the tempeh. Place pan in the middle of the oven rack and bake 20–30 minutes. Check halfway as cut size and ovens vary. It is done when crispy and browned on the outside. Remove and give another toss. Serve hot or cold.

ROTISSERIE SPICE RUB

Makes approximately ¹/₂ cup

Salt, pepper, garlic powder,
    dried oregano, dried thyme .... **1** tablespoon each
Onion powder and paprika .... **2** tablespoons each
Cayenne pepper and ground cumin .... **2** teaspoons each

Combine all ingredients in a small bowl.

Jill's Mock Chicken Salad

Serves 2 or 3

Jill Nussinow, "The Veggie Queen," dietician, teacher, and cookbook author knows what it takes to bring interest and dense nutrition to those wanting to be more healthy. This high protein recipe can be used as a salad or a sandwich filling.

Tempeh .... **8** ounces, diced into
                                              ¹/₂-inch cubes
Vegetarian chicken-flavor broth powder ...... **1** tablespoon
Pepper, freshly ground .... ¹/₄ teaspoon
Water .... ¹/₄ cup

Celery	1 stalk, chopped
Onion, finely diced	1/2 cup
Vegan mayonnaise	1/4 cup or more
Mustard, prepared	1 teaspoon
Nutritional yeast	1 tablespoon
Parsley, chopped	2 tablespoons
Salt and pepper	to taste

Steam tempeh for 15 minutes. Steaming opens up the pores to allow flavors to penetrate when using a marinade. Use a steamer basket over 1-inch water or place in a heat resistant bowl in a saucepan with a lid and add water halfway up the bowl; watch carefully.

Mix broth powder and pepper with water in a medium bowl. Add steamed tempeh and marinate for 15–20 minutes. Drain, add remaining ingredients, and gently stir to combine.

Variations: For other simple marinade choices try citrus juice, red wine, or water mixed with tamari or a dash of oil or even vegetable broth. Add any herbs or spices you like.

Spicy Nutty Tofu with Rice
Serves 4

Dr. Dotti Detwiler Kauffman shared this recipe with me. It is so good!

MARINADE

Soy sauce	3 tablespoons
Red pepper flakes	1 tablespoon
Garlic, minced	1 tablespoon
Gingerroot, minced	2 teaspoons
Sesame oil	2 tablespoons
Lemon	1, one half juiced and the other half left whole
Pickled jalapeño peppers	2, chopped
Brine from jar of jalapeño peppers	1 tablespoon

Sea salt .... dash

Sugar, sprinkle, optional

Combine all ingredients in a bowl or ziplock bag; set aside.

TOFU

Tofu, firm	**1** pound, drained and rinsed
Sesame seeds	enough to coat all sides
Vegetable oil	**2** tablespoons
Onion	**1** medium, thinly sliced
Salted or roasted peanuts, chopped	**1/2** cup
Fresh basil, sliced	**1/3** cup
Rice, cooked	**2** cups
Tomato, large	**1**, chopped

Press tofu with hands to squeeze out any liquid. Blot dry. Cut tofu into 4 serving pieces and place into a bowl or ziplock bag. Add marinade and gently toss to coat. Marinate overnight, turning tofu several times to evenly coat all surfaces.

Spread sesame seeds on a plate or pie pan. Remove tofu from marinade, reserving it, and roll tofu slices in sesame seeds to coat all sides. Set aside.

Place vegetable oil in a large skillet and sauté onion over medium heat until onions are tender, about 10 minutes. Add coated tofu slices and brown, turning once. Add all marinade, including lemon half, adding water or oil if needed; allow liquid to evaporate. Remove lemon. Add peanuts and basil; combine with tofu and heat thoroughly. Serve over rice and garnish with additional slivers of fresh basil and chopped tomato.

Maple-Ginger Baked Tofu Cutlets

Serves 4

Del Scoufe is a vegan-dedicated chef in Columbus, OH, with the Wellness Forum headed by Dr. Pam Popper.* His food is celebrated in his book, *Forks Over Knives-A Year of Meals*, and is an offshoot of the popular and important film. His recipes are versatile as to where in a meal they can be used. This recipe can be used as an entrée, a sandwich, or chopped into a salad.

Tofu, extra firm	1 pound, drained and rinsed
Bragg Liquid Aminos	4 tablespoons
Maple syrup, pure	3 tablespoons
Gingerroot, grated	3 tablespoons
Garlic	3 medium cloves, minced

Preheat oven to 375 degrees. Gently squeeze tofu to remove any liquid. Slice into 8 rectangular pieces. Place in a shallow baking pan and set aside. Prepare marinade by combining all the other ingredients. Pour over tofu and bake 20 minutes, turn over, and bake another 20 minutes. Serve with a vegetable of choice and add a salad.

Variation: For a quicker meal, heat Bragg, tamari, or soy sauce, maple syrup, and a tablespoon of vegetable oil in a skillet, add tofu and brown a bit on both sides.

*Dr. Pam Popper is an expert on nutrition and creator of The Wellness Forum that offers educational programs designed to assist in changing one's health through diet and habits.

Jambalaya

Serves 6–8

Julie Hasson, author of *Vegan Diner*, suggests making this for a fast weekday meal. Spending a lot of time in New Orleans, I could never eat their famous jambalaya. Vegan sausages by Field Roast and Tofurky Co. make it possible!

Extra-virgin olive oil	1 tablespoon
Onion	1 large, sliced into 1/4-inch crescents
Garlic	4 cloves, minced
Bell peppers, green	2, chopped
Celery	4 stalks, cut into 1/4-inch slices
Vegan sausages	2, sliced into rounds
White rice, long grain	1 1/4 cups, not rinsed
Tomatoes, organic, diced	1 (29-ounce) BPA-free can, drained
Vegetable broth	2 cups
Creole seasoning with salt (Tony Chachere's Original is classic)	1 to 3 tablespoons, to taste
Paprika, smoked	1 1/2 teaspoons
Salt and pepper	to taste, optional

Heat oil in a large saucepan with lid over medium-high heat. Add onion, garlic, bell peppers, celery, and sausage; sauté until lightly browned and slightly softened. Add rice and sauté for 1 minute more. Add tomatoes, broth, Creole seasoning, and paprika; stirring well. Bring mixture to a boil, reduce heat, cover, and simmer about 30 minutes, or until rice is tender and most of the liquid is absorbed. Add salt and pepper. Remove pan from heat and let set, covered, for 10 minutes before serving. If sausages are not available, consider using sliced vegan hot dogs.

Thai Seitan Grill

Serves 6

Vegetarian Resource Group, **www.vrg.org**, the go-to site for everything vegan, published *Vegans Know How To Party* by Chef Nancy Berkoff, EdD, RD. What better way to party than with a grilled teriyaki recipe?

THAI SAUCE

Vegan teriyaki sauce*	1/4 cup
Water	3 tablespoons
Peanut butter, creamy	1/4 cup
Red pepper flakes	1 teaspoon

Pour teriyaki sauce into a small bowl. Whisk water into sauce. Slowly add peanut butter and whisk until smooth; stir in red pepper flakes. Or mix in food processor or blender until smooth. Set aside.

*To make your own teriyaki sauce, whisk together 1/2 cup each soy sauce and water, 2 tablespoons minced fresh ginger, 2 cloves minced garlic, and 1/4 cup brown sugar. Chill for at least 30 minutes. Makes about 1 cup.

SEITAN GRILL

Seitan	2 pounds, cut into thin slices
Onion, sweet, very thinly sliced	1 cup
Thai Sauce	4 tablespoons

Preheat barbecue or indoor grill, or preheat oven to 425 degrees. Place seitan and onion on hot grill and brush with Thai Sauce. Grill, turning until heated through. Serve with more sauce on the side.

If using an oven, place seitan on a non-stick baking sheet. Brush with Thai Sauce and top with onions. Bake for 8–10 minutes or until hot.

SIX USES FOR A VEGGIE BURGER

Start the transition to plant-based foods with familiar options like a veggie burger. They are way more versatile than you think. Veggie burgers can be homemade or purchased. If purchased, I prefer the brands Morningstar Vegan Grillers, Ives, Lightlife, and Gardein. Be sure that the ingredient list is actually vegan with no cheese or egg whites.

1. Bacon Barbecue Cheeseburger
Serves 2

Veggie burgers 2
Vegan cheese (Follow Your Heart) .... 2 slices
Hamburger buns .... 2 whole grain
Onion .... 2 slices
Vegan bacon (Fakin' Bacon
   or Lightlife Bacon Strips) .... 2 strips, cooked
Barbecue sauce .... 1/4 cup

Heat burgers in a medium-hot skillet with a small spray of oil. Top each with a slice of cheese and cover until slightly melted. Warm or toast buns in a toaster oven or skillet. Assemble and add a green salad!

2. Burritos
Serves 2

Whole-wheat tortillas 2 (8-inch)
Veggie burgers 2
Pinto or black beans .... 1/2 cup, rinsed
Scallions, sliced .... 1/4 cup
Salsa .... 1/2 cup
Chili powder .... a sprinkle

Vegan cheese, grated cheddar (Daiya) .... to taste
Lettuce, dark green, thinly sliced .... ¹/2 cup
Vegan sour cream .... ¹/2 cup or more

Preheat oven to 350 degrees. Wrap the tortillas in a damp paper towel and heat to just soften or microwave in towel for 30 seconds. Cut burgers into bite-size pieces.

Place beans in a bowl and slightly mash with a fork. Add scallions, salsa, and chili powder. Lay out the tortillas and spread the mixture on one half. Put the burger pieces and cheese on top in a strip down the center. Fold one half over the filling, folding in the sides, roll up, and hold with a toothpick.

Line a baking sheet with parchment paper, place burritos on sheet, and bake about 10 minutes or until they start to brown. Serve with lettuce, extra salsa, and sour cream on the side.

3. Tacos
Serves 4

Veggie burgers .... **4**, if frozen, thaw
Taco shells **8**
Tomato .... **1** medium, chopped
Salsa .... ¹/2 cup
Vegan sour cream .... ¹/2 cup
Vegan cheese, grated cheddar (Daiya) .... ¹/2 cup

Preheat oven to 350 degrees. Cut burgers in half and place each half burger into each shell and place on baking sheet, baking until slightly toasted, about 5 minutes. Gently spoon remaining ingredients into the shells and serve.

4. Skillet Stew
Serves 6

Potatoes (white or sweet), cubed .... **4** cups
Onion, chopped .... **1** cup

Bell peppers (color of choice), chopped	**2** cups
Vegetable oil	**1** tablespoon
Tomato	**1** large, chopped
Black beans	**1** (15-ounce) can, drained
Salt and pepper	to taste
Veggie burgers	**6**, cut into bite-size pieces

Boil potatoes in slightly salted water until tender; drain. In a large skillet, sauté onion and bell peppers in oil over medium heat until almost fork tender; add potatoes, tomato, and beans and cook until heated. Remove about 1 cup of stew and purée in a blender; return to the stew. Add burger pieces and stir to heat.

5. Stir-Fry Salad
Serves 4

Spinach, fresh	**8** ounces (about 8 cups)
Bell pepper, color of choice	**1**, sliced
Parsley, fresh, chopped	**¹/₄** cup
Mint, fresh, chopped	**¹/₄** cup, optional
Vegetable oil	**2** tablespoons, divided
Veggie burgers	**4**, cut into 1-inch strips
Onion (red or white)	**1** medium, sliced
Garlic	**2** cloves, minced
Gingerroot, grated	**1** teaspoon, optional
Apple cider vinegar	**¹/₄** cup
Soy sauce	**1** tablespoon, or to taste
Hot sauce	**1** tablespoon

Place spinach in a large bowl. Add bell pepper, parsley, and mint; toss.

Heat 1 tablespoon oil in a large skillet. Add veggie burgers and brown. Remove and keep covered. Add remaining oil to skillet and sauté onion until tender. Stir in garlic and gingerroot and cook just until heated. Carefully add the vinegar, soy sauce, and hot sauce. Remove from heat and add the spinach mixture, tossing lightly with tongs until wilted. Evenly divide between 4 plates and add the burger strips to the top.

6. Salisbury Steak with Gravy

Serves 2

FAST AND EASY GRAVY

Makes 2 cups

Water	**2** cups
Vegetarian bouillon cube (Rapunzel with herbs)	**1**
Mushrooms, sliced	small can or a few fresh
Cornstarch and cold water	**2** tablespoons each
Kitchen Bouquet	**1** to 2 tablespoons, optional

Place water in a small saucepan with the bouillon and bring to soft boil. Add mushrooms. Mix cornstarch and water in a cup and add to the hot broth, stirring to thicken. Do not over boil. Stir in the Kitchen Bouquet, if using.

SALISBURY STEAK

Onion	**1** medium, sliced
Canola, safflower, or peanut oil	**1** tablespoon
Veggie burgers	**2**
Vegan Worcestershire sauce	dash, optional

Sauté onion in oil in a skillet until translucent. Remove from skillet and keep warm while browning burgers on both sides in hot skillet. Plate the "steaks," cover with onions and gravy or a dash of Worcestershire sauce. Serve with mixed vegetables and mashed potatoes.

THREE MORE BURGERS— HOMEMADE THIS TIME!

I must admit that I make most meals in a few minutes with few items. But when I was photographing *Great Chefs Cook Vegan* and met the best in the culinary world, I learned they surely like to use a lot of ingredients!

1. Vegetable Cakes

Serves 4

This recipe is for a burger or for a main dish and was developed by Master Chef Erik Blauberg, New York City, **www.erikblauberg.com**.

Olive oil	**2** tablespoons
Mushrooms, button	**8**, finely sliced
Bell peppers, red and green, finely diced	**2** tablespoons each
Jalapeño pepper, finely diced	**1** teaspoon
Garlic	**¼** clove, finely diced
Scallion or onion	**1**, finely diced
Carrot	**1**, peeled and grated
Potato	**1** small, peeled and grated
Corn	**½** cup
Broccoli	**½** cup, blanched
Lima beans	**¼** cup, blanched
Dijon mustard	**1** teaspoon
Cayenne pepper	**½** teaspoon
Bread crumbs (Panko, if possible)	**¼** cup
Salt and pepper	to taste
Flour	**½** cup
Corn oil	**2** tablespoons
Thyme	few sprigs or a sprinkle of dried

Place oil in a large skillet over medium high, heat, and stir in mushrooms, bell peppers, and jalapeño and sauté for 1 minute. Add garlic, scallion, carrot, and potato and cook 2 minutes. Remove from heat and place the mixture into a large bowl. Stir in corn, broccoli, lima beans, mustard, cayenne pepper, and bread crumbs. Season with salt and pepper. Shape into patties and dust the outside with flour and more bread crumbs, if desired. Place in refrigerator until firm or freeze until ready to use.

Heat corn oil in a skillet over medium heat and carefully place patties in the pan and cook for 1–2 minutes or until medium brown. Add thyme on top and serve on bun as a burger or as a main dish with bulgur wheat or couscous.

2. Bean Burgers

Serves 6–8

A fast-food chain in London, long ago, sold a bean burger. I had never heard of such a thing then. Even being on a business expense account, I had it for a week. This recipe was adapted from, *A Diet of For All Reasons* by Paulette Eisen, and is super easy using a can of veggie baked beans!

Vegan baked beans, canned*	1 cup
Bread crumbs	1/2 cup or more
Onion	1 medium, finely chopped
Carrots	2 medium, finely grated
Sage or parsley	1/2 teaspoon
Tomato sauce	enough to moisten mixture
Salt	to taste

In a large bowl, mash baked beans with a fork and mix in all other ingredients. Shape into patties to fit the end purpose, buns or main dish. In skillet with a small amount of oil, brown on both sides and serve.

*You can use other beans but then be sure to season with salt and pepper and any other favorite spices, perhaps garlic powder.

3. South Jersey Patties

Serves 12

Do you ask for recipes? I am always honored when asked, so I make others feel great and ask too! I just had to get this one from Freya Dinshah when I was at a picnic in New Jersey at the American Vegan Society offices.

Tomato juice	**2** cups
Onion	**1** medium to large, chopped
Carrot	**1**, sliced
Celery	**1** stalk, sliced
Nuts (raw cashews or walnuts)	$^1/_2$ cup, roasted
Soy granules*	$^1/_2$ cup
Bulgur wheat	$^1/_4$ cup
Rolled oats	$^1/_2$ cup
Salt and pepper	to taste

Preheat oven to 375 degrees. In a blender, process tomato juice, onion, carrot, celery, and nuts. Pour into a large saucepan. Stir in soy granules and bulgur wheat. On medium heat, stir until just bubbling, turning heat to low for 15 minutes or until the mixture swells and thickens. Stir in rolled oats and let stand 10 minutes.

Use about $^1/_4$ cup per patty, shaping with a fork to level top and round the sides. Bake on a greased baking sheet for about 30 minutes or until done, turning over after about 20 minutes.

*If you cannot easily find soy granules, use 1 cup refried beans instead and reduce the tomato juice to 1 cup, more or less as needed. They are easily found online.

SANDWICHES-ON-THE-GO

Consider using salad dressings, dips, and spreads on sandwiches to add tons of rich flavor. See Spreads, Sauces, Dips, and Toppings (pages 132–139) for some recipes. Jill's Mock Chicken Salad (page 108) can be used as a sandwich or wrap filling, and consider grilling a portabella mushroom as a burger.

Jannette Patterson,* a director at PETA, loves Annie's Naturals Dressing, especially the Goddess Dressing. She puts it on sandwiches as a spread and even treated me to a whole bottle to convince me. With tahini as a main ingredient I could see why.

*See **www.peta.org** for good information for the new vegan.

Collard Wrap
Serves 4

Enthusiastic Ann Crile Esselstyn is a force! She knows about good health first-hand as her husband, Dr. Caldwell Esselstyn, is a Cleveland Clinic physician.

Collard greens	**1** bunch
Hummus (made without tahini or oil)	**1/2** cup

Green onions	**2**, chopped
Cilantro or parsley, chopped	**¹/₂** cup
Carrot, shredded	**¹/₄** cup
Fresh basil	**12** leaves
Bell pepper, red	**¹/₄**, cut in thin strips
Cucumber	**¹/₄**, cut in thin strips
Lemon	**¹/₂**, zested

Put about 2 inches of water in a large skillet and bring to a boil. Choose 4 of the nicest collard leaves. Lay them flat and cut off the thick stem at end. Pile them on top of each other in the boiling water. Cover and cook for about 30 seconds to a minute. Drain.

Lay the greens flat with the thick part of the stem facing up and pat dry. Down the center spine of each collard leaf, place a row of about 2 tablespoons hummus, sprinkle with green onions, cilantro, carrot, and basil. Place bell pepper and cucumber strips on top. Sprinkle with lemon zest and generous squeezes of juice. Start with the side nearest you and gently roll into a sausage shape for a wrap.

Variation: You can make this recipe into sushi by cutting the roll into small pieces with a very sharp knife.

Peacefood Café Pumpkin and Walnut Sandwich

Serves 2

Eric Yu and Peter Lu opened a casual and busy restaurant in New York City with Eric focusing on the food and Peter on the house. This unusual sandwich seems to be what I always want to order there.

Japanese pumpkin (if unavailable, use canned pumpkin)	half
Sea salt and pepper	to taste
Olive oil	**2** plus tablespoons
Onion	**1** large, sliced
Balsamic vinegar	a splash

Agave nectar	a splash
Cashews	¼ cup
Garlic	2 cloves, roasted
Lemon juice	1½ tablespoons
Nutritional yeast	1 tablespoon
Salt	to taste
Walnuts, finely chopped	¼ cup
Dense rye bread	4 slices
Dark greens and alfalfa sprouts, if desired	

Preheat oven to 350 degrees. Sprinkle pumpkin half with salt and pepper. Roast for 30 minutes, and then scoop out and mash with a little olive oil.

Combine onion, olive oil, vinegar, and agave nectar in a saucepan and cook slowly on low heat until onion slices are caramelized, about 20 or more minutes. Set aside.

To make the cheese, place cashews, garlic, lemon juice, nutritional yeast, and salt in a blender. Blend on low until mixture has the consistency of paste. Set aside.

Using 2 slices of bread, layer cashew cheese, mashed pumpkin, caramelized onion, and walnuts. Top with greens of choice and remaining bread slices.

V-BLAT

(Vegan Bacon, Lettuce, Avocado, and Tomato Sandwich)

Serves 2

Chef Caryn Hartglass is an energetic proponent of a whole food plant diet, especially lots of greens. She created REAL, Responsible Eating and Living, a website where she shares tons of good information along with recipes and radio interviews. She loves to make this easy and fast sandwich.

Vegan mayonnaise	as desired
Vegan bacon*	**6** slices
Avocados	**2** small, peeled, pitted and thinly sliced
Tomatoes	**2** small, sliced in thin rounds
Lettuce	**2** leaves
Sesame seed buns	**2**

Spread insides of bun with vegan mayonnaise. Assemble as desired.

*Lightlife makes two types of vegan bacon; one is made with smoky soy tempeh (Fakin' Bacon) and the other is bacon-style strips made with wheat ingredients.

Diner Egg and Olive Salad Sandwich

Makes 3 cups or 6 sandwiches

There was nothing, and I do mean nothing, that I loved more than having an egg and olive salad sandwich with my mom at the counter of the diner. It gives easy protein, and with whole grain bread and good greens, you have all you need.

Vegan mayonnaise .... **1 cup**
Mustard, prepared .... **1 teaspoon**
Salt and pepper .... to taste
Onion, finely chopped .... ¼ cup
Green olives, pimento stuffed, sliced .... ¼ cup
Tofu, firm or extra firm .... **1** (16-ounce) package,
                                                                            drained
Whole-grain bread (Ezekiel 4:9 with sesame seeds)
Lettuce, any kind, but this is the one time I want nostalgia iceberg lettuce

Mix mayonnaise, mustard, salt, and pepper into a large bowl. Add onion and olives and mix. Crumble tofu on top of the mixture by squeezing through your fingers. With a spatula, lift up the dressing from the bottom and carefully blend. Build the sandwich.

PASTA AND PIZZA

The more pasta is cooked, the higher the glycemic index rating will be, so cook until just tooth-tender, also known as al dente. You can request this in restaurants as well. In most pasta recipes, beans can be substituted for the pasta.

Chef Adams' Linguine Bolognese

Serves 4

Yes, Bolognese—the term vegans run from when they see it on a menu! Chef Robert Adams oversees the biggest vegan Thanksgiving feast in the country at Parizäde near Duke University in Durham, NC. The red wine as an ingredient makes this so authentic in taste.

Olive oil	**2** to **4** tablespoons
Vegan margarine	**2** tablespoons
Mushrooms	**2** pounds, quartered
Garlic	**4** cloves, chopped
Onion	**1** medium, diced
Carrot	**1** medium, diced
Thyme	**2** tablespoons
Red wine	**2** cups

Zucchini	1 medium, diced
Garbanzo beans	1 (15-ounce) can, drained and rinsed
Tomato sauce	1 quart
Salt and pepper	to taste
Whole-wheat linguine	8 ounces

Heat a large saucepan over medium-high heat; add oil, margarine, and mushrooms. Do not crowd mushrooms; if necessary, make in batches to sear and not steam. Cook until they start to brown then stir and cook some more, adding garlic, onion, and carrot. Add a small amount of hot water, if sticking. Simmer until onions are done; add thyme and red wine. Cook until the liquid is reduced by about two-thirds. Add zucchini, beans, and tomato sauce; season and simmer 10 minutes. Set aside and keep warm until pasta is ready.

Cook pasta according to package directions and serve with sauce.

Nava's Baked Macaroni and "Cheese"

Serves 4–6 adults or 6–8 children

Nava Atlas is the author and illustrator of many books. Her website is a go-to place for good information and recipes, **www.vegkitchen.com**.

Whole-wheat elbow pasta	**1** pound
Silken tofu	**1** package
Vegan margarine	**2** tablespoons
Vegan cheddar-style cheese, grated	**1**^{1}/**2** cups, firmly packed
Bread crumbs, fresh	**1** cup
Salt	to taste

Preheat oven to 400 degrees. Cook pasta in salted water for 8–10 minutes until al dente; drain and set aside. While pasta is cooking, purée tofu in a food processor or blender until perfectly smooth. Transfer to a saucepan and add margarine and cheese. Slowly bring to a simmer, stirring often, and cook over low heat until cheese is melted. Combine with pasta in a large bowl and then place in a baking dish and top with bread crumbs; salt to taste. Bake for 20 minutes or until top is golden and crusty.

Erin's Pizza On-The-Go

Serves 4

Erin Schrode is a young woman on the go, see **www.erinschrode.com**. She promotes a world view in relation to global sustainability, environmental education, and conscious lifestyle choices.

Garlic	1 to 2 cloves
Salt	to taste
Tortillas, brown rice	4 large
Bell pepper, green	1 medium, sliced
Red onion	1 medium, sliced
Tomatoes, heirlooms, if possible	3 medium, sliced and quartered
Olives, mix of kalamata and niçoise, pitted, chopped	1 cup
Fresh basil	1 bunch
Pepper	to taste
Basil, oregano, rosemary, and thyme	1 teaspoon each
Extra virgin olive oil	optional

Preheat oven to 450 degrees. On a cutting board, mash garlic and salt together, sliding side of knife back and forth to create a paste consistency. Bake tortillas for 5–7 minutes until slightly crispy. Remove from oven and spread with thin coating of garlic paste. Place bell pepper and onion on garlic, cover with tomato slices and sprinkle olives and basil over the top. Add salt, pepper, and seasonings, to taste. Bake on top shelf of oven for 10–12 minutes until edges are golden brown, checking periodically to ensure top does not burn. Drizzle with olive oil, if desired, and serve.

Variation: Add vegan cheese before adding vegetables.

Josephine's Elegant Party Bowtie Pasta
Serves 4

Josephine Hall is elegant and her food is elegant. This might seem like an ordinary pasta dish, but it is not! Tasting is believing. She serves it with a mesclun salad with sliced fresh pears and toasted walnuts.

Onion	1 large, chopped
Extra virgin olive oil	1/2 cup, divided
Salt and pepper	to taste
Garlic	1 clove, crushed
Portobella mushrooms, sliced	2 to 3 cups

Farfalle (bowtie) pasta	1 pound
Truffle oil	optional, but encouraged

In large skillet, sauté onion in small amount of olive oil over moderate heat, until softened. Add a sprinkle of salt and pepper. Reduce to low heat and add garlic; cook 1 minute, taking care not to burn. Transfer onion and garlic mixture to a large serving bowl.

Cover bottom of skillet with a bit more oil, turn heat to high and add mushrooms; sauté to brown before they "sweat." It is best to do this in batches, adding a bit of oil each time, so that each mushroom receives the maximum heat. Lightly salt and pepper each batch. Transfer to serving bowl and toss with the onion mixture.

Meanwhile, boil pasta in salted water 8–10 minutes until al dente; drain. Add pasta and onion-mushroom mixture back into the pot and cook over medium heat for 1 minute. Return to serving bowl and serve. To make it even more elegant, drizzle with some truffle oil.

SPREADS, SAUCES, DIPS, AND TOPPINGS

Take these seriously! They contribute big flavor and pleasure to the foods we eat. The surprising thing is that they are usually quite interchangeable.

A SPREAD, often used on crackers, bread, and wraps, can also be thinned with water or soy milk and used over a salad or vegetables.

Don't think of SAUCE as only a sauce. It can become a sandwich or wrap dressing. For a great cheese sauce, see Broccoli with "Cheese" Sauce (page 96).

DIPS are more than something to scoop onto a cracker. Dips, and even salsas, can be spread on sandwiches and used with side vegetables.

A TOPPING for a salad can also be a topping for a sandwich, soup, or vegetables.

Chickpea Havarti Cheese Spread

Makes 2 cups

Jo Stepaniak is an author and a book editor. For this recipe she states, "It is high in protein as well as flavor. This zippy vegan spread is great for sandwiches and snacks. If you use canned beans, it's a snap to prepare."

Water	1 cup
Chickpeas (cooked or canned)	2 cups (rinse and drain, if canned)
Cashews, raw	$^1/_2$ cup
Nutritional yeast	$^1/_3$ cup
Lemon juice	$^1/_4$ cup
Onion powder	2 teaspoons
Salt	1 teaspoon
Dried dill weed	$^1/_2$ teaspoon
Whole celery seeds	$^1/_2$ teaspoon
Garlic powder	$^1/_2$ teaspoon

Place all ingredients in a blender and process until completely smooth. Pour into medium saucepan and cook over medium heat, stirring frequently until very thick, about 15–20 minutes. Remove from heat and let cool for about 30 minutes. Cover and refrigerate 8–12 hours before serving. This spread can be stored in the refrigerator for a week.

Reprinted by permission from Jo Stepaniak, *The Ultimate Uncheese Cookbook* (Summertown, TN: Book Publishing Company, 2003).

Lentil Walnut Pâté

Makes 3¹/₂ cups

Roberta Schiff is head of the Mid-Hudson Vegetarian Society in the Rhinebeck, NY, area. In traveling and speaking around the country about becoming vegan, she treats her audience with this recipe to show how great some favorite non-vegan dishes can be in a vegan version. This is her "liver pâté."

Onions	**2** very large (about 2 pounds), sliced
Olive oil	**2** tablespoons
Lentils, brown, uncooked	**1** cup, rinsed
Water	**2** cups
Walnuts	**³/₄** cup, lightly toasted
Scallions	**2** or 3, sliced
Tamari or soy sauce	**1** to 2 teaspoons

This is a recipe that is best done in a food processor.

Sauté onions in olive oil in a covered skillet over medium heat and then medium low as they become tender, for about an hour. Yes, an hour! Start the onions while making the rest of the recipe.

Add lentils and water to a saucepan, bring to boil, cover, reduce heat, and cook to tender, about 20 minutes. Add lentils, sautéed onions, walnuts, and scallions to a food processor. Process until desired texture, chunky or smooth. Add tamari. Serve with rye bread, crackers, or Romaine lettuce scoops.

Olive Walnut Spread
Makes 4 cups

Chef Del Sroufe works with the Wellness Forum in Columbus, OH. His book, *Forks Over Knives-A Year of Meals,* is an off-shoot of the popular film of the same name. He shares this versatile spread recipe that is good on sandwiches, wraps, crackers, or bread.

Tofu, extra firm	1 (12-ounce) package
Almond butter	6 tablespoons
Miso	3 tablespoons
Garlic	3 cloves, peeled
Dill	2 teaspoons
Walnuts, toasted and coarsely chopped	1 cup
Kalamata olives, halved	1 cup

This is a recipe that is best done in a food processor.

Place all ingredients, except walnuts and olives, in a food processor; blend until smooth and creamy. Transfer mixture to a bowl and add walnuts and olives.

Lee Hall's Baba Ghanouj
Serves 6

Lee Hall* is the legal mind of Friends of Animals. She eagerly shares this eggplant dip or spread that is a classic dish on every table in the Middle East.

Eggplant	1 large
Tahini	1/4 cup
Lemon	1, juiced
Garlic	1 clove, pressed or finely minced
Sea salt	1/2 teaspoon
Pepper	a pinch, optional
Olive oil	1 1/2 teaspoons, divided
Tomato	1, chopped, optional
Fresh parsley	1 sprig, optional

Preheat oven to 400 degrees. Push a fork into the skin of eggplant in several places and roast directly on oven rack for 55 minutes, or until soft throughout. Place a baking pan below rack to catch drops of juice. Turn off oven and leave door open, allowing eggplant to cool on the rack for 15 minutes. Remove from oven and carefully cut off stem. Cut in half and scoop out all pulp and mash in a bowl or shallow baking dish. Add tahini, lemon juice, garlic, salt, pepper, if desired, and just 1 teaspoon of olive oil, mashing the mixture thoroughly. Place mixture in a shallow bowl and drizzle with the remaining olive oil. Garnish with chopped tomato or a sprig of fresh parsley, or both. Serve with pita chips, crostini or flatbread.

*Lee Hall wrote one of the most unique books about animal rights with In Their Own Terms.

Macadamia-Cashew Nut Cheese

Makes about 1 1/2 cups

Chef Angel Ramos, Candle 79 in New York City, offered this recipe for a cheesy alternative for a creamy ricotta.

Cashews, raw	1/2 cup
Macadamia nuts, raw	1/2 cup
Lemon juice	3 tablespoons
Grapeseed oil	2 tablespoons
Nutritional yeast	2 tablespoons
Sea salt	to taste
Water	1/2 cup

In separate bowls, cover cashews and macadamia nuts with water and soak overnight, or for a minimum of 8 hours. Drain and wash nuts until water rinses clear. Blend all ingredients, except water, in a blender, adding water as needed until mixture is a creamy consistency.

Parm Sprinkle

Makes 2¹/₂ cups

Sprinkle this mixture on any dish where you would use Parmesan cheese. It is good on everything—soups, vegetables, pasta, stir-fries, French fries, and even on sandwich fillings.

Sesame seeds	**2** cups
Nutritional yeast	**¹/₂** to **³/₄** cup (taste after ¹/₂)
Onion powder	**1** teaspoon
Garlic powder	**1** teaspoon
Salt	**1** teaspoon

Preheat oven to 325 degrees. While watching very closely, lightly toast sesame seeds to slightly browned. Note that seeds contain a lot of oil and can burn very easily. Process sesame seeds with remaining ingredients in a blender until mixture is crumbly. It will keep for weeks in the refrigerator.

Inger's Norwegian Caraway Cheese Spread

Serves 6

My Norwegian friend, Inger, shared this recipe. Adding other herbs and spices to this base recipe can create many soft cheese spreads. The caraway can be eliminated if it does not fit with the new flavors. For a Boursin-like cheese, add some finely minced parsley, dill, garlic, marjoram, thyme, basil and perhaps a touch of white wine or a pinch of vegan Parmesan cheese.

Tofu, extra firm	**14** to **16** ounces, cut into 3 pieces

Lemon	**1**, juiced and strained
Sea salt	**1** to 2 teaspoons, or to taste
Caraway seeds	**1** tablespoon or a $^1/_2$ teaspoon of ground

Combine tofu, lemon juice, salt, and seeds in blender or food processor, blending to a smooth paste. Store at least 5 hours or overnight in refrigerator to blend flavors and thicken. Use as spread on crackers or as a vegetable or fruit dip.

Chef Adam's Chickpea Pesto

Makes 3$^1/_2$ cups

Chef Adam Rose is a gifted chef who shared this recipe that gets raves from his customers at Il Palio Restaurant in Chapel Hill, NC.

Basil leaves	**3** cups loosely packed
Baby spinach leaves	**1** handful
Garlic	**3** cloves, peeled
Extra virgin olive oil	$^1/_2$ cup
Salt and pepper	**1**$^1/_2$ teaspoons each

Combine above ingredients in a food processor and set aside.

Chickpeas, canned	4 cups, drained and rinsed
Extra virgin olive oil	6 tablespoons, divided
Lemon	1, juiced
Salt and pepper	1 1/2 teaspoons each

Using a food processor, purée chickpeas, 1 tablespoon olive oil, lemon juice, and half of pesto mixture. Add remaining olive oil, as needed, and remaining pesto. Pulse until mixture is of spreading consistency. Add salt and pepper. Spread on a favorite artisan bread and have a happy experience.

Sour Cream

Makes 2 cups

Toni Fiore* is host of Delicious TV's *Totally Vegetarian* on PBS. She often answers the question about how to have dairy products without really having dairy products. This is the way not to miss it!

Tofu, firm, regular or silken	1 package
Extra virgin olive oil	1/3 cup
Lemon juice, fresh	1/4 cup
Apple cider vinegar	1 1/2 tablespoons
Sea salt	2 teaspoons

Place all ingredients in a blender and process until smooth and creamy. Store in an airtight container for up to a week. For another idea, add some horseradish. This is especially good with sliced red beets or borscht.

*Toni Fiore is also the author of *Totally Vegetarian: Easy, Fast, Comforting Cooking for Every Kind of Vegetarian.*

Judy's Herb Sandwich Spread

Makes 3/4 cup

Flavor is what makes most sandwiches memorable. My Nashville friend is the best sandwich maker on the planet. Just one of her secrets—herb spread!

Celery seed, dried onion powder, basil,
oregano, parsley, thyme, rosemary or
sage, marjoram, and fennel seeds .... **1** tablespoon each
Red pepper flakes, sea salt, and pepper .... **1** teaspoon each

Mix all ingredients together in a jar. If desired, 1 minced small garlic clove can also be added. Cover with water just to the height of the mixture. Soak at least 8 hours or overnight on the counter for maximum swelling. Once soaked, it can be refrigerated.

Use as a spread on bread, sandwiches, or to flavor-pack salad greens by first adding a bit of olive oil, grapeseed oil, or other vegetable oils.

Raw Cashew Whipped Cream
Makes 1 1/2 cups

Beverly Lynn Bennent's contributions to vegan cooking are impressive. See **www.veganchef.com** to discover her books, among them, *The Idiot's Guide to Vegan Cooking*. This recipe is from her "Dairy-Free Desserts" column in the fabulous and essential *VegNews Magazine*.

Cashews, raw .... **1 1/2** cups
Medjool dates* .... **6**, pitted
Water, filtered .... to cover
Orange juice .... **1/3** cup

Place cashews and dates in a medium bowl. Cover with filtered water and set aside to soak 2–3 hours or overnight. Drain and discard water. Transfer to a food processor or blender and add orange juice. Blend for 1–2 minutes to form a very smooth and creamy topping. Serve with pies, tarts, or on top of fresh fruit. Store in refrigerator in an airtight container.

*Medjool dates are the very large meaty variety, and wonderful snacks on their own.

SNACKS! YAY!

Popcorn with Nutritional Yeast

Use an air popped version or a microwave brand without oil. I love Bearitos Organic brand, lightly salted, 25 calories a cup. Alternate layers of popcorn and sprinkles of nutritional yeast.* This snack is crisp, tasty, and a bit cheesy. If you must have "butter," melt about a tablespoon of vegan margarine in the microwave for about 10 seconds and drizzle each time just before the nutritional yeast.

*NOW Nutritional Yeast Flakes by Red Star is most popular. It is an inactive yeast and does not cause any issues for those with a yeast sensitivity. It is fortified with additional B vitamins such as a B-12.

1. Spicy Mixed Nuts
Makes 3 1/2 cups

These nuts are a spectacular snack for any occasion or no occasion at all! They are also a great topping to a salad. Take as a party hostess gift!

Oil (peanut, sunflower, or canola) .... **2 tablespoons**

Nut mixture (peanuts, cashews, almonds, and sunflower seeds)	1 pound
Garlic	1 clove, crushed
Paprika and chili powder	1/2 teaspoon each
Soy sauce or tamari	1 tablespoon

Heat oil in a skillet over low heat and add the nuts, stirring for about 5 minutes or until golden. Add garlic, paprika and chili powder. Stir a couple minutes more. Add soy sauce to coat nuts. It will evaporate instantly. Remove pan from heat. Cool.

2. Fat-Free Hummus

Makes 2 cups

Hummus is a chickpea dip from the Middle East and is high in vitamin C, iron, protein, and fiber. Use this as a base and alter garlic and lemon juice, to taste. Most recipes use creamy tahini, which is high in fat. Also consider using black beans or edamame in another version.

Chickpeas	1 (15-ounce) can, drained, reserve liquid
Garlic	1 to 2 cloves
Lemons	2 medium, juiced
Liquid from canned beans	1/4 cup
Soy sauce or Bragg Liquid Aminos	1 teaspoon

Combine all ingredients in a food processor or high-powered blender until smooth. Serve with veggies, crackers, or baked pita chips.

3. Salsa with Baked Pita Chips

SALSA

| Tomatoes, chopped | 1 1/2 cups or 1 (14.5-ounce) BHA-free can |

Bell pepper, red, chopped	¹/₂ cup
Onion (red or white), chopped	2 tablespoons
Jalapeño pepper	1, finely chopped
Garlic	1 clove, finely chopped
Lime	1, juiced
Parsley or cilantro, chopped	2 tablespoons
Salt	¹/₄ teaspoon

Combine all ingredients in a bowl and allow to sit for several hours or overnight in the refrigerator. Flavors blend in magic ways when allowed to set. If you prefer a hotter salsa, add a few drops of hot sauce.

BAKED PITA (OR TORTILLA) CHIPS

Pita whole-wheat rounds, 4-inch or tortillas, (whole wheat, sprouted grain, white, or yellow), 6- to 8-inch	1 (8-ounce) package
Canola oil	enough to lightly spray or brush chips
Salt	to taste
Paprika or another seasoning of choice, optional	

Preheat toaster or standard oven to 350 degrees. Cut pitas or tortillas into triangles with a pizza cutter or sharp knife. Arrange a layer on an ungreased baking sheet. Lightly spray or brush with oil. Lightly sprinkle with salt and other seasoning, if using. Bake for about 5 minutes, turn over with tongs, and bake until crispy, just a few more minutes. Sometimes, they do not need to be turned if the baking trays are rotated midway.

4. Edamame

Edamame, organic, shelled or in pods

Boil in water about 5 minutes. Salt the water and then test afterward to see if more is desired. Eat warm or cooled.

5. Seasoned Kale Chips

These are super nutritious and super low in calories. Try them with nutritional yeast, salt, or Old Bay Seasoning.

Kale, fresh	1 bunch
Olive oil	enough to lightly coat leaves
Nutritional yeast, salt, or	
Old Bay Seasoning	light coating

Preheat oven to 350 degrees. Cover a baking sheet with parchment paper. Wash and completely pat dry the kale leaves, or use a salad spinner. Strip the leaves from the hard stems by tightly wrapping thumb and forefinger at wide end of the stem, and holding tight, push the leaves forward to the other end. Tear leaves into bite-size or chip-size pieces. Rub some oil in your hands and massage each leaf. Sprinkle with seasoning of choice and lay out on the baking sheet. Bake until very slightly browned at edges, perhaps 10–15 minutes. Cool.

Note: Nutritional yeast adds tons of nutrients and gives a cheesy taste. Try this way at least once!

6. Red and Green Frozen Grapes or Roasted Grapes

Grapes can freeze very elegantly. It is all in the plating when serving. Place selected bunches of washed red and green seedless grapes on a plate and place in the freezer until frozen. Simply pull off one by one for eating and feel them dance in your mouth! I can barely believe how good this is.

Roasting: Wash grapes and cut in half. In a bowl, drizzle with the smallest amount of olive oil along with a sprinkle of salt and a favorite herb, perhaps thyme. Spread over a baking sheet with parchment paper and roast at 400 degrees until soft and golden. I especially like to add these to fresh spinach with some crumbled vegan bacon, but they can stand as a side all on their own.

DESSERTS

We all love desserts! When you feel the need to splurge, try one of these fabulous options.

Creamy Oats Sundae with Maple Tofu Whip

Serves 2–3

From Fran Costigan's *More Great Good Dairy Free Desserts Naturally.* Who could imagine that soaked rolled oats are so luscious.

Rolled oats	¹/₃ cup
Nondairy milk	¹/₂ cup
Nuts (almonds, walnuts, peanuts, etc.), chopped	2 tablespoons
Fresh or dried fruit or berries, chopped	to taste
Soy yogurt	¹/₂ cup, optional
Maple or brown rice syrup	to taste, optional
Chocolate chips	2 to 4 tablespoons, optional
Maple Tofu Whip topping	

Combine oats and milk in covered container and refrigerate for 8–24 hours. The longer they soak, the creamier the oats will be. Before serving, add nuts, fruit, and any optional items. Spoon into parfait glasses, either mixed together or in layers. Top with Maple Tofu Whip.

Maple Tofu Whip

Makes 1 cup

This recipe is so versatile—keep it in mind for some of the desserts you already make, or for pie topping, ice cream topping, or perhaps just on some toast!

Tofu, firm	8 ounces, drained
Neutral oil, such as canola	1 tablespoon plus 1 teaspoon
Maple syrup	5 tablespoons
Vegan granulated cane or maple sugar	2 tablespoons
Vanilla	2 teaspoons
Fresh lemon juice	2 teaspoons
Salt	$^1/_4$ teaspoon
Cinnamon	$^1/_8$ teaspoon

Crumble tofu into a blender or food processor and process for 1 minute. Add remaining ingredients and process until very smooth, about 5 minutes depending on your machine. Stop periodically to clean sides with rubber spatula. Place in a covered container and refrigerate 3 hours or longer to blend flavors. The whip will thicken slightly as it chills.

4 Easy Pies Buffet

BANANA DREAM PIE

Serves 6–8

Jennifer Raymond, with this recipe from her book, *Fat-Free & Easy*, made me a memorable cook countless times. It is extraordinarily light and just the right flavors to beg the next bite.

Cane sugar	$^1/_2$ cup
Cornstarch	**6** tablespoons
Nondairy milk	**2** cups
Salt	$^1/_2$ teaspoon
Vanilla	**1** teaspoon
Tofu, firm	**8** ounces
Bananas	**2**, peeled and sliced
Quick Crust, prebaked graham cracker crust	**1** (9-inch)

Mix sugar and cornstarch in a saucepan; stir in milk and salt. Cook over medium heat, stirring constantly until mixture becomes a very thick pudding. Remove from heat and stir in vanilla.

Drain tofu and blend in food processor until smooth and fluffy. Add to pudding and gently blend with a spatula until smooth. Place sliced bananas into rounds over the crust. Spread pudding mixture on top. Refrigerate until completely chilled, at least 1 hour.

PEANUT BUTTER AND CHOCOLATE VELVET PIE

Serves 6–8

What is there about the combination of these two flavors? And, at least 70% of chocolate has good anti-oxidants and peanut butter is full of protein.

Pie crust, whole wheat	1 (8-inch)
Chocolate chips, dairy-free	2 cups
Peanut butter	1¾ cups
Tofu, firm	1 (16-ounce) package
Soy milk, vanilla	½ cup or more as needed

Bake pie crust according to package instructions. Carefully melt chocolate chips in microwave oven for 10 seconds, stir, and reheat if necessary to completely melt. Add all ingredients, except crust, to a food processor or high-powered blender. (If only a regular blender is at hand, mix as well as possible in a bowl and then add to the blender in appropriate mixable batches then combine all batches.) Mixture should be very thick. Pour into pie crust and refrigerate until chilled or at least 2 hours.

PECAN PIE

Serves 6–8

Chef Eric Tucker in San Francisco created this recipe for his restaurant, Millennium. He brings this recipe out every holiday and so do I!

Pecans	2½ cups, coarsely chopped
Maple syrup	⅓ cup
Brown rice syrup	⅓ cup
Vanilla	1 tablespoon
Gingerroot, minced	1 tablespoon
Sea salt	¼ teaspoon
Arrowroot	2 teaspoons
Soy milk	⅓ cup
Flaxseeds, ground	3 tablespoons
Pie crust of choice, prebaked	1 (9-inch)

Preheat oven to 350 degrees. Spread pecans on a baking sheet and toast for 12–15 minutes. Watch carefully as the nut oils can easily burn. Place pecans in a large bowl and set aside.

In a medium saucepan, combine maple syrup, brown rice syrup, vanilla, gingerroot, and salt. Simmer for 5 minutes then remove from heat and cool to room temperature. Combine arrowroot, soy milk, and flaxseeds with the maple syrup mixture; pour into a blender and process until smooth. Pour mixture over pecans and mix well. Pour into pie crust and bake for 30 minutes, or until the filling is firm. Cool.

PUMPKIN PIE

Serves 6–8

Paulette Eisen initially created a wonderful little cookbook called, *A Diet for All Reasons*, as an accompaniment to an important video lecture of the same name by Dr. Michael Klaper When I was first vegan I longed for a good Thanksgiving pumpkin pie, but all I found required eggs. It was exciting to find this book and this recipe which super satisfies, surprises all non-vegans, and could not be any easier.

Soy milk	$1^1/2$ cups
Cornstarch	$^1/4$ cup
Pumpkin, cooked, canned is fine	$1^1/2$ cups
Cane sugar	$^1/4$ cup
Salt	$^1/2$ teaspoon
Cinnamon	1 teaspoon
Ginger, ground	$^1/2$ teaspoon
Cloves, ground	$^1/8$ teaspoon
Pie crust, whole wheat or regular, unbaked	1 (9-inch)

Preheat oven to 375 degrees. In a large bowl, whisk soy milk and cornstarch until smooth. Blend in remaining ingredients, except pie crust. Pour into crust and bake 45 minutes.

"Mound Bar" Sundae

Serves 1

I grew up selling Mound Bars to the truck drivers at my parents' diner. I never forgot the wonderful combo of the dark chocolate over the soft coconut. This dessert is fast and easy when you need a last minute dessert.

Vanilla soy ice cream or coconut
   milk ice cream..amount desired
Fran Costigan's Ultimate Chocolate Sauce (see below)
Coconut flakes for topping

FRAN COSTIGAN'S ULTIMATE CHOCOLATE SAUCE
Makes 1¹/₂ cups

Water..	¹/₂ cup
Cocoa powder,* unsweetened......................	³/₄ cup
Vegan granulated sugar...............................	¹/₂ cup
Salt..	¹/₄ teaspoon
Maple syrup	¹/₂ cup
Canola oil...	2 tablespoons
Vanilla..	1 tablespoon

Pour water into a small saucepan and bring to a boil. Remove from the heat. Combine cocoa, sugar, and salt in the bowl of a blender or food processor. Pulse a few times to mix. With the motor running, pour 6 tablespoons of the hot water through the feed tube. Stop and clean the sides with a rubber spatula. Add the maple syrup, oil, and vanilla. Process about 1 minute until smooth. The sauce will be thin, but thickens as it cools. Refrigerate until ready to use.

*There are two main kinds of unsweetened cocoa powder, natural (acidic, deep flavor) and Dutch-processed (alkalized, mild flavor). Fran suggests the Dutch-processed for this recipe. I prefer to make this with Hershey's Natural Unsweetened Cocoa Powder.

Good Ole, Plain Ole Chocolate Pudding
Serves 4

Jennifer Raymond, cookbook author and devoted vegan, was at the North American Vegetarian Conference when I was a new vegan. I have depended on her contributions since. This pudding is from her recipes that were in Dr. Neal Barnard's *Food For Life*.

Soy milk or rice milk	1 1/2 cups
Cornstarch	3 tablespoons
Cocoa powder	1/4 cup
Maple syrup, pure	1/4 cup
Vanilla	1/4 teaspoon

Whisk all ingredients together in a medium saucepan. Cook over medium heat, stirring constantly until pudding is thickened, usually until first stages of boiling. Pour into 4 individual serving dishes.

Sometimes, I add 1 teaspoon of dry instant coffee with the ingredients for a mocha tasting pudding, or more often, a bit of peanut butter.

Easy Skillet Drop Biscuits and Hot Berries

Serves 4–6

I photographed this recipe by Debra Daniels-Zeller, for *Vegetarian Journal*. This dish is something else! And, it goes together so quickly.

BERRY MIXTURE

| Mixed berries (blueberries, raspberries, blackberries) | 5 cups |

Water	....	$^1/_2$ cup
Cane sugar	....	**2** to **4** tablespoons, depending on sweetness of berries
Lemon juice	....	**2** tablespoons
Lemon zest	....	**2** teaspoons
Arrowroot or cornstarch	......	**1** tablespoon

DROP BISCUIT BATTER

Soy milk	....	$^1/_3$ cup
Lemon juice	....	**1** tablespoon
Flour	....	**1** cup
Cane sugar	....	$^1/_4$ cup
Baking powder	....	**2** tablespoons
Baking soda	....	$^1/_2$ teaspoon
Lemon zest	....	**1** tablespoon
Vegan margarine, cold	....	**2** tablespoons

Place berries, water, sugar, lemon juice, zest, and arrowroot in a large heavy skillet and simmer over medium heat. Lower heat to medium-low and cook for 5 minutes, stirring frequently. Set aside.

To make biscuits, combine milk and lemon juice in a small bowl. Blend flour, sugar, baking powder, baking soda, and lemon zest in a medium bowl. Mix well. Using a pastry blender or fork, cut margarine into mixture until small pieces. Stir in milk mixture until dough is just moistened.

Bring berry mixture back to a simmer and drop biscuit mixture from a teaspoon onto berries, starting around the outside of the pan then toward the center. Cover and continue simmering over low heat for 30 minutes. When inserted toothpicks come out clean, they are done.

Del's Shortbread Dough – Master Recipe
Makes 24–28 cookies

Chef Del Sroufe, works with the Wellness Forum in Columbus, OH. Vegans sometimes do not know how to bake without eggs and when it comes to cookies at holidays it is especially so. This is a fail-safe one that should be considered a master recipe, one that stands alone but can also be a starting point for many more options.

Vegan margarine, room temperature	**1** pound
Organic cane sugar	**1** cup
Vanilla	**1** tablespoon
Unbleached white flour	**4** cups, divided
Nuts of choice	**1** cup, optional

Preheat oven to 350 degrees. Using a mixer with a paddle blade, beat margarine and sugar until light and creamy. Add vanilla and beat another minute. Add flour, 1 cup at a time, mixing well. Using small scoop, drop cookies onto ungreased baking sheet. Top with nuts and bake 20 minutes or until golden brown.

JAM THUMBPRINTS
Del's Shortbread Dough—Master Recipe (see above)
Jam of choice

Preheat oven to 350 degrees. Prepare shortbread dough. Dip your thumb in flour and make an indentation in each cookie. Bake 10 minutes. Remove from oven and fill each cookie with jam. Return to oven and bake another 10 minutes.

SHORTBREAD CUT-OUTS

Del's Shortbread Dough—Master Recipe (page 153)
Colored or chocolate sprinkles

Preheat oven to 350 degrees. Prepare shortbread dough. Wrap and chill dough for at least 1 hour. Roll dough on floured surface so it is about $^1/_3$-inch thick. Using cookie cutters, cut into desired shapes. Place on ungreased baking sheet and decorate with sprinkles. Bake 15 minutes or until golden brown.

SNICKERDOODLES

Del's Shortbread Dough—Master Recipe (page 153)
Organic cane sugar .... $^1/_2$ cup
Cinnamon .... 1 teaspoon

Preheat oven to 350 degrees. Prepare shortbread dough. Combine sugar and cinnamon. Using a medium scoop, form cookies and dip tops into cinnamon-sugar mixture. Place on ungreased baking sheet. Bake 18 minutes or until golden brown.

Peanut Butter Cups

Makes approximately 48 pieces

Jane Belt, a home economist in Columbus, OH, gave me some of these during her usual Christmas trip to New York City, and she was pressed into making more while she was here. So easy, so fast!

Vegan margarine	**1** cup, melted
Graham cracker crumbs	**2** cups
Confectioner's sugar	**2** cups
Peanut butter, creamy	**1**$^1/_4$ cups, divided
Semisweet chocolate chips, dairy free	**1**$^1/_2$ cups

Combine all ingredients, except the chocolate chips and $^1/_4$ cup of peanut butter, in a bowl until well blended. Spread and press into bottom of an ungreased 9 x 13-inch baking pan. Place chocolate chips and remaining peanut butter in a microwave-safe bowl and heat for 10 seconds or slightly more, if needed. Stir in order to check softness. Pour over the mixture in the pan and evenly spread over top. Refrigerate until completely cooled, about an hour. Cut into 1$^1/_2$-inch squares or cups using a round cookie cutter.

Mignardises

Makes approximately 80 half-teaspoon pieces

These bite-size tastes are served at the end of a meal. I joked with Chef Charlie Trotter that he used these to ease the pain of the check, as they appear with the bill!

Cashew butter, raw	1 cup
Maple syrup	1 cup
Cocoa powder	1 cup
Vanilla seeds, scraped	1/2 teaspoon
Raw soy sauce, called nama shoyu (regular soy sauce if unavailable)	1 tablespoon

Combine ingredients in a food processor. Pour into shallow covered container and refrigerate about 4 hours. Using a 1/2 teaspoon, scrape chocolate truffle mix into small balls. Fill or roll pieces with cocoa, spices, cayenne pepper, mint, nut pieces, sesame seeds, sugars, dried fruit or treats, and shape as desired.

Addictive Energy Bars

Makes approximately 20 pieces

Melissa Maly shares this recipe from her New Jersey restaurant, Wildflower, earthly vegan fare. **www.wildflowervegan.com**.

Quick oats	**6** cups
Chocolate chips, dairy free	**1** (12-ounce) package
Coconut, shredded	**1** cup
Sunflower seeds	**1** cup
Walnuts, chopped, and almonds, sliced	**1** cup each
Cranberries, dried, or raisins	**1** cup
Nut butter of choice	**2** cups
Agave syrup and brown rice syrup	**1** cup each
Vanilla	**1** tablespoon plus 1 teaspoon

Preheat oven to 350 degrees. Mix dry ingredients in a large bowl and liquid ingredients in a small bowl. Add the liquid ingredients to the dry; mix well. Pour batter into 9 x 13-inch baking pan and press evenly with spatula until mixture is well distributed. Bake for 18–20 minutes until top is a light brown. Remove from oven and cool.

Once fully cooled, cut into bars the size that suits your purpose. Keeps at room temperature for weeks; can be frozen for extended time.

Fast Cookies for School Lunches

Makes 24–30 cookies

Karen Campbell is the wife of Dr. T. Colin Campbell, known for "The China Study." She has listened to more lectures on nutrition than perhaps anyone else on the planet. She offers these cookies as a healthy option for a standard treat.

Maple syrup	$^1/_3$ cup
Almond milk	$^1/_3$ cup
Cocoa	$^1/_4$ cup
Peanut butter, smooth	3 tablespoons
Vanilla	1 teaspoon
Oats	1 $^1/_2$ cups
Walnuts	$^1/_4$ cup, optional

Combine maple syrup, milk, and cocoa in a saucepan. Bring to a boil then simmer for 3 minutes. Add peanut butter and stir until dissolved. Remove from heat and add vanilla, oats, and walnuts, stirring well until cool enough to handle. Using a teaspoon, form into small cookies about 1-inch in diameter. No baking necessary! Store in airtight container.

Jane's Mango Ice Cream Pops

Serves 6

Jane Velez-Mitchell of CNN and HLN is proud to share her easy dessert.

Mangoes	2, peeled and cut into chunks
Banana	1, broken in half
Vegan cream cheese	3 tablespoons
Soy milk to an inch of the top of the fruit	
Stevia	1 packet, optional

Blend all ingredients. Pour into 6 popsicle molds or small paper cups with added sticks. Freeze for about 4 hours or overnight. Squeeze sides to unmold.

FANCY VEGAN: FOR THE GOOD TIMES

The big question I get so often is, "What do you eat at Christmas and other holidays?" The answer is, "Most of what you eat, just without the animals." Of course, I know they think that if I am not eating the animals there is nothing to eat! Yet, meat, poultry, or fish are only one part of the meal. The sides of peas, corn, beans, squash, vegetables, greens, and all the others seem to have little meaning when they are the most nutritious items on the table!

There are many dishes to serve now that mimic the old standard recipes that used animal and dairy products. There are endless dishes that are flavorful and new. Look over the recipes that follow to fully understand how anyone would be thrilled to have such experiences at the dinner table.

MENU TEMPLATE

One dinner, many occasions—whether it is for a winter holiday, Sunday dinner, special celebrations, romantic dinner, or just a fancy dinner for no reason at all, you have only to use your imagination to make it a wild success!

Only the colors and table decorations need to be different to reflect the occasion, like red and green for Christmas, orange and brown for Thanksgiving, blue and silver for Hanukkah, crayon colors for birthdays, black and silver or gold for New Year's Eve, and related colors for other holidays or the season of the year. Remember, even a picnic can be fancy!

If one menu is mastered, you always have a fancy meal you can do without panic and then you can enjoy yourself in the process. File all details in a folder so you can remember all the wonderful things you did to use the next time!

Thanksgiving Dinner

Serves 6

Drinks: Rum-spiked warm cider, (some unspiked for those not
wishing alcohol), red or white wine, fresh orange juice spritzer

Appetizers: Edamame (page 143), sliced carrot rounds, Spicy Mixed
Nuts (page 140)

Bread: No need as puffed pastry on the "turkey" serves for bread

Salad: Tossed mixed green salad with apple slices and Sweet Spicy
Mustard Dressing (page 55)

Soup: Not needed for this menu

Main Course: Holiday "Turkey" with Bread Stuffing and Gravy (see
facing)

Sides: Stovetop Candied Sweet Potatoes (page 74), Dixie Diner's
Creamy Coleslaw (page 96), corn

Dessert: Pumpkin Pie (page 149) with Raw Cashew Whipped
Cream (page 139)

Coffee or Tea: Have soy creamer available as it does not separate in
hot liquids as regular vegan milks might.

After Dinner Treats: Soft ginger candies, 70% cocoa chocolate bar squares (store purchased)

After Dinner Drinks: Cointreau (orange liqueur) or Poire William (pear liqueur), coffee, and/or tea

Goodie Bag: Spicy Mixed Nuts (page 140). Place desired amount into a white paper sandwich bag, fold over the top once, punch a hole in the middle, push an orange, brown, or gold ribbon through and tie nicely. Perhaps add an orange or yellow leaf cutout included in the tie.

Holiday "Turkey" with Bread Stuffing and Gravy

Mushroom Bread Stuffing	1 recipe (see below)
Chicken-like Gravy	1 recipe, divided (page 162)
Seitan (chicken-flavored or regular), pieces or strips	1 package
Puffed Pastry (Pepperidge Farm Brand is vegan)	2 sheets

Mushroom Bread Stuffing

Serves 8

Vegetable oil	1 tablespoon
Onion, chopped	1 cup
Celery, sliced	1 cup
Mushrooms, button, sliced	3 cups
Walnuts, chopped	1/4 cup
Bread	5 slices, cut into 1/2-inch cubes
Fresh parsley, finely chopped	1/2 cup
Sage, pepper, and salt	1/4 teaspoon each
Thyme and marjoram	a pinch of each
Very hot water or vegetable stock	about 1 cup

Add oil to large saucepan, sauté onion, celery, and mushrooms for 5 minutes. Add walnuts, cover, and cook over medium heat until mushrooms are brown, about 10 minutes. Add a bit of vegetable stock if more moisture is needed for browning. Add bread and seasonings. Stir in water or stock a little at a time until dressing obtains desired moistness. Check seasonings and adjust. Allow to meld for about 2 minutes.

Chicken-like Gravy

Makes 2 cups

Vegan bouillon cube* **1**
Water .... **2** cups
Cornstarch and cool water .... $^1/_4$ cup each, stirred together

* Other options are to use bouillon powder or 2 cups vegetable broth

Heat water in a small saucepan, add bouillon and dissolve. Pour in cornstarch mixture and stir until thickened. Do not boil.

To Assemble

Preheat oven to 400 degrees. Place rack in lower position. Following instructions on puffed pastry box, roll out first pastry sheet on a floured surface. Place it on a baking sheet, shaping into an oval to create the bottom of the "turkey."

Spread bite-size pieces of seitan over the pastry. Moisten with $^1/_4$ cup gravy. Pile mounds of bread stuffing high over the seitan into the desired shape and drizzle $^3/_4$ cup gravy over mixture. Roll out and stretch the second sheet of puffed pastry over the top stuffing, gently shaping and smoothing the top to the lower edges as needed. Press the pastry neatly around the bottom edge. Cut away any extra dough.

Using the scraps of leftover dough, fashion some leaves or other shapes and place artfully on the "turkey." Attach with a brush of soy milk for glue. Brush top of "turkey" with a touch of soy milk to help with browning. Bake on lower rack for about 15–20 minutes until browned and heated through. Allow to rest a few minutes and carefully slide onto a platter for cutting at the table into 1-inch slices. Be sure each slice has all the components; top generously with remaining gravy.

Christmas or Winter Holiday Dinner

Serves 6

Drinks: Alicia's Warm Spicy Wine (page 51), sparkling white wine
(alcoholic and nonalcoholic) with three floating pomegranate
seeds, cranberry juice with seltzer and lime slice

Appetizers: Stuffed Grapes (see below), Popcorn with Nutritional
Yeast (page 140)

Bread: No need as bread is in the soup and main course.

Salad: Arugula salad, pomegranate seeds, toasted walnuts, Balsamic
Vinaigrette (page 54)

Soup: Chef's Vegetable Broth (page 61) and float a buttered and
minced parsley-topped star-shaped (use cookie cutter) whole-
grain bread toast

Main: Cashew Nut Roast with Parsley Stuffing and Gravy
(page 164)

Sides: Fluffy Mashed Potatoes (page 87), platter of vegetable sides

Desserts: Del's Shortbread Dough-Master Recipe (page 153) made
into Christmas cookies, and/or a buffet of pies from 4 Easy Pies
(pages 146–149)

Coffee and Tea: Offer a variety of specialty holiday options

After Dinner Treats: Mignardises (page 156)

After Dinner Drinks: Framboise (raspberry liqueur), Créme de Menthe
(green mint liqueur), coffee, tea, Hot Chocolate (page 52)

Goodie Bag: More cookies in a little box or clear cellophane bag
with a holiday ribbon.

Stuffed Grapes

Multi-cookbook author, Robin Robertson, created this easy, fun, and festive idea.

Large green seedless grapes .... **3** per person
Walnuts, ground, or nut of choice
Jam (black raspberry or flavor of choice)

Cut off the tops of the grapes and a slice a little off the bottom if making vertical ones. Sense the center of gravity so they will stand sturdy. Or, cut in half lengthwise. Hollow out a bit of flesh to make room for the filling with a small spoon or the tip of a knife. Mix ground nuts and jam, coaxing the two ingredients together until well-mixed. Put a small amount into each grape cavity. Tasty!

Cashew Nut Roast with Parsley Stuffing and Gravy

This is a favorite recipe from celebrated British cookbook author Rose Elliot, *Vegetarian Christmas* (HarperCollins Publishers London). I also make this when I want to show-off. There are only a few ingredients; it is just the way they are placed in the loaf pan that makes it seem like a big deal.

CASHEW NUT ROAST

Vegan margarine	$1/4$ cup
Onion	**1** large, sliced
Cashews, raw	**1**$1/2$ cups
Bread (white or whole grain), crusts removed	**4** slices
Garlic	**2** large cloves

Water or light vegetable stock	about **1** cup
Salt and pepper	**1/4** teaspoon each
Nutmeg, grated	**1/8** teaspoon
Lemon juice	**1** tablespoon

Heat oven to 400 degrees and line an 8 x 4 x 2-inch loaf pan with a long strip of parchment paper for bottom and end sides, using a bit of the margarine to anchor the paper to the pan. In a medium saucepan, melt the margarine and add the onion; cook about 10 minutes until tender but not browned. Set aside.

Combine the cashews, bread, and garlic in a food processor. Add mixture to the onion and then the water or stock, salt and pepper, nutmeg, and lemon juice. Set aside while making the stuffing.

PARSLEY STUFFING

Bread crumbs, white	**1/2** cup
Vegan margarine, softened	**1/4** cup
Onion	**1** small, grated
Thyme and marjoram, dried	**1/2** teaspoon each
Parsley, chopped	**1** cup, packed
Parsley sprigs	

Combine all the stuffing ingredients together in a small bowl. Set aside.

To Assemble

Divide the nut roast mixture in half. Spread half evenly in the bottom of the pan. Carefully spread all of the stuffing mixture on top and cover with the other half of the nut roast mixture. Dot with margarine. Bake for 30 minutes. If top browns too quickly, loosely cover with parchment.

Cool for a few minutes in the pan then slip a knife around the sides. Place a plate on top of the pan and carefully turn both over to have roast come out onto the plate, bottom-up. Garnish with parsley sprigs.

Make Chicken-like Gravy (page 162) to serve over the top.

Special Sunday Dinner

Serves 6–8

Drinks: Beer, white wine, Instead-of-Soda Soda (page 50)

Appetizers: Lentil Walnut Pâté (page 133)

Bread: No need with breading on the "chicken" and crackers with the soup.

Salad: Victoria's Incredible Kale Salad (page 69)

Soup: Fast Horseradish Tomato Soup (page 65) with whole grain crackers

Main Course: Southern Fried "Chicken" (see below)

Sides: Fluffy Mashed Potatoes (page 87) or Better For You Fries (page 89), Broccoli with "Cheese" Sauce (page 96)

Dessert: Easy Skillet Drop Biscuits and Hot Berries (page 151) or Good Ole Plain Ole Chocolate Pudding (page 150)

Coffee and Tea:

After Dinner Treats: Cantaloupe cubes with toothpick or small fruit kabobs skewered with small cubes of cantaloupe, watermelon, and grapes

After Dinner Drinks: Dessert wine like a small glass of port ("crusty" ones are vegan, ask clerk), Kirsch (cherry liquor), coffee, tea, pitcher of fast nonalcoholic sangria of orange juice/ grape juice/ seltzer water (1:4:4) with added slices of lemon, orange, apple, or peach.

Goodie Bag: Mason jars filled with Original Granola (page 41) with a copy of the recipe, including Banana Milk (page 42) recipe. Tie ribbon or raffia around the neck. Package both in a small colorful gift bag.

Southern Fried "Chicken"

This crispy "chicken" takes only about 5 minutes for the first prep day, 15 minutes for the second prep day, and about 30 minutes to complete on the third day. You can combine day two and day three prep if you marinate only 3 hours instead of overnight.

Chef Kevin Dunn created this wonderful recipe to teach his students at Grand Rapids Community College's Secchia Institute for Culinary Education. He teaches upcoming chefs that plant meals are important for their future work. This dish is often on the menu in their formal dining room.

DAY ONE: PREPARE TOFU

Tofu, firm .... 1 (16-ounce) package

Cut tofu into 4 slices; cut again into triangles. Place in covered container and freeze overnight.

DAY TWO: MARINATE

Sage, dried .... 1 tablespoon
Garlic powder, onion powder,
   and pepper .... $^1/_2$ teaspoon each
Rosemary, thyme, sage, paprika,
   and turmeric .... $^1/_4$ teaspoon each
Nutritional yeast .... $^1/_2$ cup
Garlic .... 4 cloves, smashed
Salt .... $^3/_4$ teaspoon
Vegetable broth .... 1$^1/_2$ quarts

Combine all ingredients and add to tofu. Marinate at least 3 hours or overnight for best results.

DAY THREE: DREDGE AND COOK

Flour	**6** cups
Paprika	**2** tablespoons
Dried sage, turmeric	**1** tablespoon each
Dried thyme, garlic powder, marjoram	**1/2** teaspoon each
Pepper	**1** teaspoon
Cayenne pepper	**1/4** teaspoon
Baking soda	**4 1/2** teaspoons
Salt	**1** tablespoon plus 1 1/2 teaspoons
Beer	**1 1/2** quarts

Combine all dry ingredients and separate into 3 flat bowls. Add beer to 1 batch, a little at a time, whisking well to blend. Dip a finger in batter to check consistency. Batter should just thinly coat your finger.

Next create 3 dredging stations: dry batch, batter, dry batch. Add canola or peanut oil to large skillet (about 1/2 inch deep) and turn heat to medium-high. Dip each tofu piece in dry flour mixture, then batter, and lastly coat with dry flour mixture. Immediately fry first side of tofu pieces until brown and crispy. Turn and brown the other side. Drain on paper towels.

RECOMMENDED RESOURCES

Visit **www.virginvegan.com** for an extensive and fabulous resource list.

NUTRITION BOOKS

Barnard, Neal D., M.D. *21-Day Weight Loss Kickstart: Boost Metabolism, Lower Cholesterol, and Dramatically Improve Your Health.* New York, NY: Hachette Book Group, 2011. **www.pcrm.org, www.nutritionland.org**

Campbell, T. Colin, PhD and Thomas Campbell II, MD. *The China Study: Startling Implications for Diet, Weight Loss, and Long-Term Health.* Dallas, TX: BenBella Books, 2006. **www.tcolincampbell.org**

Esselstyn, Jr., Caldwell B. *Prevent and Reverse Heart Disease.* New York, NY: Penguin Book Group, 2008. **www.heartattackproof.com**

Freston, Kathy. *Veganist: Lose Weight, Get Healthy, and Change the World.* New York, NY: Weinstein Books, 2011. **www.kathyfreston.com**

Fuhrman, Joel, M.D. *Eat to Live: The Revolutionary Formula for Fast and Sustained Weight Loss.* Boston, MA: Little, Brown and Company, 2003. **www.drfuhrman.com**

Moran, Victoria and Adair Moran. *Main Street Vegan: Everything You Need to Know to Eat Healthy and Live Compassionately in the Real World.* New York, NY: Tarcher, Penguin Group, 2012. **www.mainstreetvegan.net**

RECIPE BOOKS

Atlas, Nava. *Wild About Greens.* New York, NY: Sterling, 2012. **www.vegkitchen.com**

Costigan, Fran. *More Great Good Dairy-free Desserts Naturally.* Summertown, TN: Book Publishing Company, 2006. **www.francostigan.com**

Pierson, Joy, Angel Ramos, and Jorge Pineda. *Candle 79 Cookbook: Modern Vegan Classics from New York's Premier Sustainable Restaurant.* Berkeley, CA: Ten Speed Press, 2011. **www.candle79.com**

Raymond, Jennifer. *Fat-Free & Easy: Great Meals in Minutes.* Calistoga, CA: Heart & Soul Publications, 1995, 1997.

Ronnen, Tal. *The Conscious Cook: Delicious Meatless Recipes that Will Change the Way You Eat.* New York, NY: HarperCollins Publishers, 2009. **www.talronnen.com**

Stepaniak, Jo. *The Ultimate Uncheese Cookbook: Delicious Dairy-Free Cheeses and Classic "Uncheese" Dishes.* Summertown, TN: Book Publishing Co., 2011. **www.vegsource.com**

ANIMAL RIGHTS AND THE ENVIRONMENT

Baur, Gene. *Farm Sanctuary: Changing Hearts and Minds about Animals and Food.* New York, NY: Touchstone, 2008. **www.farmsanctuary.com**

Brown, Jenny with Gretchen Primack. *The Lucky Ones: My Passionate Fight for Farm Animals.* New York, NY: Avery Books, Penguin Group (USA), 2012. **www.woodstockanimalsanctuary.org**

Hall, Lee. *On Their Own Terms: Bringing Animal-Rights Philosophy Down to Earth.* Darien, CT: Nectar Bat Press, 2010. **www.friendsofanimals.org**

Joy, Melanie, Ph.D. *Why We Love Dogs, Eat Pigs and Wear Cows: An Introduction to Carnism.* San Francisco, CA: Canari Press, 2010.

Robbins, John. *Diet for a New America: How Your Food Choices Affect Your Health, Happiness, and the Future of Life on Earth.* 2nd ed. Tiburon, CA: H.J. Kramer, 1998.
No Happy Cows: Dispatches from the Frontlines of the Food Revolutions. Berkeley, CA: Conari Press, 2012. **www.johnrobbins.info**

MAGAZINES

American Vegan. The American Vegan Society. **www.americanvegan.org**

VegNews. VegNews Media. **www.vegnews.com**

Vegetarian Journal. The Vegetarian Resource Group. **www.vrg.org**

Vegetarian Times. Cruz Bay Publishing. **www.vegetariantimes.com**

Vegetarian Voice. North American Vegetarian Society. **www.navs-online.org**

MEDIA: DVDS AND ONLINE TV

Delicious TV. "Vegan Hotspot." Hosted by Linda Long. New York: **www.veganhotspot.com** and "Totally Vegetarian" and "Vegan Mashup." Recipe videos **http://www.youtube.com/user/TotallyVegetarian** or on iTunes.

Klaper, Michael, MD. "A Diet for All Reasons." **www.doctorklaper.com**. DVD.

PETA. "Glass Walls." Narrated by Paul McCartney. Darien, CT: PETA, 2010. DVD.

Wolfson, Marisa Miller. "Vegucated: 3 People, 6 Weeks, 1 Challenge." **www.getvegucated.com** DVD.

LEADING WEBSITES AND BLOGS

VEGETARIAN SOCIETIES

The Vegetarian Resource Group. **www.vrg.org**

North American Vegetarian Society. **www.navs-online.org**

VEGAN ONLINE EDUCATIONAL

www.robinasbell.com and **www.vegsource.com**

ANIMAL RIGHTS GROUPS

www.wikipedia.org/animalrightsgroups

www.sanctuaries.org

VEGAN ATHLETES

Brendan Brazier **www.brendanbrazier.com**

Robert Cheeke **www.veganbodybuilding.org**

MISCELLANEOUS WEBSITES

Alcohol Beverage Guide, vegan-friendly **www.barnivore.com**

Big City Vegan, Shop for great cruelty-free products, gifts, etc. **www.bigcityvegan.com**

Happy Cow. Guide for vegan restaurants world-wide. **www.happycow.com**

INDEX

LINDA LONG has had a lifelong relationship with the food and hospitality industry and has been a committed vegan for more than three decades. Trained as a home economist, she has had a varied career in the academic, corporate, and media communities, with a strong emphasis in fashion, food, and nutritional topics. She authored and photographed the award-winning *Great Chefs Cook Vegan* (Gibbs Smith, 2008), a book featuring 25 of the nation's top chefs applying their talents to plant foods. Linda writes and photographs stories for vegetarian magazines, *Vegetarian Journal* and *American Vegan,* and is a sought after food photographer for other cookbook authors. She photographed the recipes for the *New York Times* award-winning *The Conscious Cook* by Tal Ronnen. She is the host/NYC producer for Vegan Hotspot, a web-based TV show by Delicious TV that spotlights vegan restaurants in New York City.

Photo © 2012 Dan Demetriad

Linda has lectured at universities on vegan nutrition and as a member of the James Beard Foundation (JBF), she gave the first book talk on a vegan subject at the James Beard House. She is also a member of International Association of Culinary Professionals (IACP), New York Women's Culinary Alliance, and the American Society of Media Photographers (ASMP).

Metric Conversion Chart

Volume Measurements		Weight Measurements		Temperature Conversion	
U.S.	**Metric**	**U.S.**	**Metric**	**Fahrenheit**	**Celsius**
1 teaspoon	5 ml	1/2 ounce	15 g	250	120
1 tablespoon	15 ml	1 ounce	30 g	300	150
1/4 cup	60 ml	3 ounces	90 g	325	160
1/3 cup	75 ml	4 ounces	115 g	350	180
1/2 cup	125 ml	8 ounces	225 g	375	190
2/3 cup	150 ml	12 ounces	350 g	400	200
3/4 cup	175 ml	1 pound	450 g	425	220
1 cup	250 ml	2 1/4 pounds	1 kg	450	230

Tempeh
Tofu
Cashews
RED
PEPPER
Miso
VANILLA
OLIVE
OIL
Lemon
Garlic
Tomato
maple syrup
CAYENNE
SALT
SOY
Black Pepper
Mint
OATS